HALIFAX CHAMPION

Black Power in Gloves

Robert Ashe

Formac Publishing Company Limited
Halifax

Formac Publishing Company Limited acknowledges the support of the Culture Division, Nova Scotia Department of Tourism, Culture and Heritage. We acknowledge the financial support of the Government of Canada through the Book Publishing Industry Development Program (BPIDP) for our publishing activities.

We acknowledge the support of the Canada Council for the Arts for our publishing program

---

Visual Credits
All photographs are from the Downey family collection except where noted below:
Mary Bricker: p. 123, p. 131
Chantal G. Désilets: author photo (back cover)

Library and Archives Canada Cataloguing in Publication

Ashe, Robert
Halifax champion : black power in gloves / Robert Ashe.

Includes bibliographical references and index.
ISBN10: 0-88780-677-5
ISBN13: 978-0-88780-677-3

1. Downey, Dave 2. Boxers (Sports)—Canada—Biography. 3. Blacks—Nova Scotia—Halifax—History. 4. Nova Scotia—Social conditions—1945-1991. I. Title.

GV1132.D69A84 2005 796.83'092 C2005-904553-1

Formac Publishing Company Limited
5502 Atlantic Street
Halifax, Nova Scotia B3H 1G4
www.formac.ca

Printed and bound in Canada

CONTENTS

ACKNOWLEDGEMENTS

Many people helped me tell this story about a fascinating period in my hometown, taking the time to share their experiences and memories.

I conducted more than 40 interviews, an even mix of face-to-face and telephone. I snapped on my tape recorder in all manner of places and circumstances. A sparsely furnished apartment reeking of stale urine. An empty, backstreet restaurant in Kitchener, Ontario. A Halifax seniors' residence amid the whirr of powered wheelchairs. A musty boxing gym in Brantford, Ontario. The laundry room of a North End Halifax housing complex. The VIP room of a plush hotel on the waterfront. A legion hall. A law office. A farmhouse. Living rooms. Coffee shops. Sports bars.

Three men I interviewed have since passed away. Promoter LeRoy 'Rocco' Jones died in 2000, Brantford manager and trainer Frank Bricker in 2002 and boxing executive Murray Sleep in 2003. All will be missed.

There were roughly 25 hours of recorded interviews with David Downey. All took place in his home or in the North End apartment of his brother, Billy, an uncommonly pleasant man who frequently supplied detail his younger brother could not.

Incalculable hours were spent in libraries — most in the National Library in Ottawa — sifting through clippings or staring into screens as spools of blurred newspaper microfilm slid past. The *Chronicle-Herald* and *Mail-Star*, Halifax's only dailies at the time, supplied substantial information. Magazines and books were also very useful, notably *The Ring Record Book and Boxing Encyclopedia*, widely considered the sport's most trustworthy resource.

Such a spread of sources resulted in a glut of information and the inevitable factual contradictions. Some inconsistencies were never completely resolved. Such is the nature of a sport never known for its dedication to documentation, too often trusting recollected "facts" of men of age and ego who, earlier in their lives, absorbed many, many punches to the head.

Other people also merit my appreciation in this effort.

Staff at Formac Publishing — especially senior editor Elizabeth Eve, who understood and supported this book from the beginning — did a fine job. Professor Roger Bird, of Carleton University's School of Journalism, offered some wonderful insights. Librarians in Ottawa and Halifax were extremely helpful no matter how many other demands they were juggling. And my wife, Brenda, and son, Adam, were always patient during those many evenings when I disappeared to God knows where to work on this project. Thank you all.

Robert Ashe

September 2005

INTRODUCTION

> *"For me, to be a boxer was my outlet dream, and you have to live what you want to be."*
>
> — David Downey

I approached David Downey one afternoon in August 1998 with the idea of writing a book about his life. It was a typical foggy Halifax day, a surface calm with moist air hinting at a summer storm. I had little trouble finding him. He was still in the North End working-class neighbourhood where he grew up, living now in the last of a series of sober two-storey row houses off Maynard Street. I knocked twice. A slender child of about 10 opened the door and called for his grandpa. Seconds later a man peered over the top of the child's head.

"Dave Downey?" I asked.

The question was unnecessary. The round, amenable face had hardly aged since the 1970s, when it appeared often in the local daily newspaper. The eyes still held a glint, and the hair, while thinned a little, was still dark. The body however, in its 57th year, was plainly no longer that of a middleweight. The shoulders were too thick, the forearms too large, and the belly stretched the limits of a navy blue T-shirt.

"You got him," he beamed.

On the doorstep I launched into my proposal, hastily dropping names, talking at twice my usual tempo. Downey smiled and nodded, then ushered me into his living room where he settled deep into a chesterfield that long ago had conformed to the shape of his rear. I sat in a chair six feet away. A faded portrait of Malcolm X hung on the wall above the TV.

I continued to pitch my idea, racing through what I knew about his career and the lively period in which he fought. I told him I was intrigued — yet puzzled. The book would examine why things turned out the way they did, but I stressed it would be an honest portrait of the man and his times. Warts and all. "I'm not going to be your publicist."

He nodded again.

Sitting erect, Downey turned his head away from me slightly, keeping his eyes fixed on mine. He held this pose for several seconds and said nothing. Then he frowned. There were things that he, too, did not understand, he finally offered.

The summer storm was about to hit.

"I wish somebody would tell me why I'm not in that hall of fame," he said. "It's just not right!"

It had been more than 20 years since he last fought, and still the Nova Scotia Sport Hall of Fame had not seen fit to honour him. Tremendously unjust, he repeated. To make matters worse, just recently he had been overlooked yet again, thanks to what he considered an obstinate selection committee headed by long-time local sportscaster Pat Connolly.

While it is a pleasing enough attraction, the Nova Scotia Sport Hall of Fame is not the Smithsonian. A non-profit entity supported by private donations and the provincial government, the hall is guided by a board of directors and tended by a small administrative staff. It opened in 1964 in an industrial structure next to the Halifax Forum and has since changed its name and location numerous times. For the last several years it was on the main floor of the Centennial Building in downtown Halifax, a few blocks up from the harbour. That site was easily missed, save for a life-sized copper statue of an early twentieth-century boxer near the entrance. Inside, the layout and the lighting gave the displays a hushed, peculiar reverence. Recently it moved yet again, this time to the Halifax Metro Centre complex.

The hall did not hold its first induction ceremony until 1980. As of 1998, 381 athletes, teams and builders had been honoured.

Boxer David Downey was not among them.

This despite the battery of local men and women who, over the years, had written to the selection committee to plead for his induction. Advocates included prominent politicians, community leaders and friends. Few athletes could claim a more consistent and resolute campaign on their behalf.

Halifax mayor Walter Fitzgerald cited Downey's "hard work, talent and determination." Gordon Earle, a local Member of Parliament and long-time acquaintance, described him as "a gentleman and role model for many black athletes." Wayne Adams, a provincial environment minister, wrote of a "colourful" and "controversial" career that delighted thousands of fight fans.

Wilfred Jackson, executive director of the Nova Scotia Home for Coloured Children, chided the hall for not recognizing "one of our living legends in the ring." And Patrick Curran, a provincial court employee who played baseball against Downey around 1960, recalled, "Dave stood out as a sportsman. He was probably the friendliest person in the league."

The longer we chatted the deeper Downey receded into his chesterfield. At one point he sprang up, darted from his living room for several minutes and returned with a mound of loose papers balanced atop an old, frayed album. There used to be a lot more clippings and stuff, he explained, but much of it was lost in a house fire some time back. We flipped through the album for almost half an hour. Downey watched intently as I quietly read some of the clippings. When I placed them back on the coffee table he leaned forward.

"I was middleweight champion for all that time and they still haven't put me in the hall of fame," he bristled. "Why? I just can't figure it out. That's the way it's been for me in this city."

He was born into a family of fighters. But while several of his brothers boxed proficiently, none had the pure skill of David, the youngest, who fought professionally from 1960 to 1977. He was Canadian middleweight champion from September 1967 to May

Dave Downey, Canadian middleweight champion, in mid-career (c. 1973).

1975, save for a four-month gap in 1970 that almost everyone in Halifax benevolently forgets. During his lengthy reign he defended his title just five times, losing two of those fights. In all, his official record was 23 wins, four losses, two draws and one no decision. Despite his abundant talent, he was never ranked higher than the top 50 or so in the world.

Yet behind these understated numbers rests a remarkable story. It is a story of a proud, strong-willed man whose calling coincided with one of the most dynamic periods in Halifax's history — a time of conspicuous, extensive economic and cultural transition, which saw the emergence of the city's black population as a social and political force.

Joan Jones, a prominent Halifax activist of the 1960s and 1970s, remembers its vigour and excitement. "I had more of a feeling of purpose and accomplishment during that period than I think I ever had since. It was a time when things were happening." Her former husband, Burnley 'Rocky' Jones, also a prominent figure of the era, reflected many years later, "Back then we had idealism and optimism."

Downey's career also paralleled another cultural shift — the decline of local boxing.

Prizefighting had been for generations a splendid and vicious part of Halifax's character, passionately driven by a rich mixture of local men — affluent and nearly destitute, principled and corrupt, wise and inept, heroic and sad. They drew blood and were themselves bled dry. The sport's practitioners both amused and alarmed mainstream Halifax. Wildly popular in the 1940s and 1950s, over the next two decades boxing would creep towards the margins — its decreasing relevance neither recognized nor understood by local fighters or others married to the sport.

Even so, in the Halifax of the 1960s and 1970s boxing still mattered.

"The fight game in Halifax always drew a very, very interesting cross-section of the community," says Halifax-born Gerald Regan, premier of Nova Scotia in the 1970s. "Because of the fact we always produced very good fighters of African-Canadian descent, you'd get quite a number of people from that community who'd attend the fights. You'd also get working-class people, and a very large number of businessmen who would have been amateur fighters, perhaps. Diverse backgrounds that probably wouldn't have mixed together otherwise."

"It was like a large social club," agrees former Halifax mayor Walter Fitzgerald. "Everybody knew everybody."

Halifax cabby Bill Godley was a fight-night regular at the Halifax Forum, for decades the city's largest arena. "When there was a fight card announced, you'd go to the Forum and get your tickets. Fight night was *my* night. I was married and money was tight, but when it comes to the fights — that's it. I'm gone! Don't ask me to paint a wall or fix the door. It's fight night! You'd see friends that you haven't seen since the last fight. Between the fights you'd go out and walk around the corridor. There'd always be a couple of scraps — black on black. [They'd] be goin' at it — and I mean *goin' at it.* The cops pretty well knew what was goin' on. A lot of the guys would have a bottle in their pocket."

By design and by quirk, David Downey asserted control over his career in a manner different from most other fighters. Although a handful of Nova Scotian boxers ended up with buildings bearing their names and plays depicting their lives, many spent their careers merely lining the pockets of others — then died young. Downey refused to be exploited by local promoters, although few, if any, had such intent. He also resisted public sentiment and the local press, both of which contended he did not fight frequently enough. The suggestion continues to chafe Downey.

From his perspective, few understood the value of the Canadian middleweight championship and fewer still knew of the sacrifice it required. His lack of public acceptance progressively troubled and confused Downey. During his career he stated publicly once — and privately many times — that the city simply did not seem to like Downeys.

This was a curious thesis. Especially so because one older brother, Graham, during this period launched a lengthy run as a Halifax alderman. Another brother, Billy, became a very successful club owner in the 1970s. And their mother was one of the most respected women in all of North End Halifax.

The lament nonetheless had *some* merit, if only to cast light into the shadows of his city — the shadow of Halifax's central importance, now faded; the shadow of racism stretching back to the eighteenth century; and the shadow of a white boxer named Blair Richardson, a middleweight champion whose extraordinary popularity was an albatross for Downey from beginning to end.

It is with Richardson that this book begins.

1

PERFECT

On a mid-June day in 1967 a Nova Scotian icon gripped the telephone in his Boston apartment and chose his words carefully. "The viciousness is gone," boxer Blair Richardson, 26, told sportswriter Aubrey Keizer of the *Cape Breton Post.*

It was time to retire.

He had not fought in 11 months, although there were discussions about world title fights with both Dick Tiger and Emile Griffith. The Canadian and British Empire middleweight champion, Richardson had been scheduled to defend his Canadian title later that month in Glace Bay, Nova Scotia. He felt physically ready for the fight, but his heart was not in it. He said it would be unfair to his fans in Cape Breton if he fought and gave anything less than his best.

"At one time fighting was everything to me. Now I want to do other things. I haven't the motivation, and there was no point in continuing. There were no more horizons."

Articulate, polite, handsome, blond, white and religious, Richardson was adored by his province and revered by its media. He was also enormously respected by boxing insiders.

"He had that special presence about him and incredible luminescence," wrote the *Chronicle-Herald.* "And because he was interested in people he had the knack of making everybody he came in contact with feel important. You sense that anything nice you say about him might not fit. If you said he was the All-Canadian Boy, you'd be wrong because he was better than that. You'd be wrong in saying he was the son every father wanted because he was even better than that."

"He was such a gentleman," reflects Harris Sullivan, a Halifax sports broadcaster during the 1960s. "He was one of these people who was almost too good to be true."

A great many people agreed.

Johnny Condon, publicity director at New York's Madison Square Garden, once proclaimed "there is nothing wrong with boxing that a few more Blair Richardsons can't cure. Boy, what an advertisement for the fight game."

Veteran broadcaster Pat Connolly, of Dartmouth, Nova Scotia, once labelled him "your ideal Canadian," a young man who ignited the public's imagination. "He was a very intelligent and very charming individual. He was a sort of media darling. He was this big handsome Hollywood Adonis guy who could hit like hell and so he was very, very exciting and very, very attractive. But beyond that, his relationship with the media was wonderful because he was always there and accessible. We counted on him always to say something intelligent and he brought another dimension to the game — that dimension of thoughtful expression."

Keith Paris, a Halifax welterweight, recalls he used to stay at Richardson's home when he was in Cape Breton. "He was A1. I'd go there and Blair'd say, 'Take my room' and 'Look after my friend.' He treated me just like part of the family."

Peanuts Arsenault, a tough welterweight from Prince Edward Island, is more succinct. "Blair Richardson was perfect."

Blair Richardson was born in 1940 in Sydney, Nova Scotia, and raised working-class in nearby South Bar, a village along the Sydney River where coal and steel dominated. Blair's father, Leland, started working at the coke ovens in 1936. The job never granted an easy day, but through the years it supplied a decent house in a respectable neighbourhood for himself, his wife and their three sons.

Polite and deferential to adults, Blair was a good all-round athlete but an indifferent student. He rarely studied. "What took him so far was his memory," Leland speculated. His taste for boxing emerged in his mid-teens under a retired fighter named Johnny Nemis, from neighbouring New Waterford. "He lived to train," said Leland of his eldest son. "Every day he'd do roadwork or go to the gym. All the time it was gym, gym, gym, skipping, the punching bag out in the garage, running to the lake and back."

While his popularity spanned the Maritimes, his core support came from fellow Cape Bretoners — men who smelled of the mines and made no apology for it. They screamed loudest for blond Blair, as if his thunderous fists and thrilling victories could vanquish black lung disease and the other horrors in their lives. Busloads from Sydney and Glace Bay rolled into Halifax for Richardson fights, which frequently attracted crowds of more than 5,000 and filled the Halifax Forum, the city's largest arena.

A Richardson match often followed a simple but dramatic pattern. He started slowly, then, on the brink of defeat, in the late rounds, he would summon a crashing right. Most fights ended there. Often his hand shattered with the force. At least six times during his career he would break or fracture his hands, mostly the right. This vulnerability was no secret. In July 1962 the widely-read *Boxing Illustrated* wrote that he might overcome his "handicap of brittle hands" with added maturity and the correct placing of his punches. Nevertheless, it would be a career-long issue. Halifax fight official Murray Sleep remembers that Richardson "had the smallest pair of hands for a middleweight that I ever saw in my life."

Small hands or not, when Richardson's monster stirred, opponents fell. Plainly he possessed killer instinct, the gloried gift that *Globe and Mail* boxing writer Stephen Brunt describes as "the type of inner anger that allows a fighter to hurt another man and then, rather than backing off, move in and complete the task." In 11 years as a professional he won 45 matches — 36 by knockout — and lost only seven. At one point he had 16 straight knockouts and was the sixth-ranked middleweight in the world.

Richardson won his first pro fight in 1956 when he was just 16. By 1959 he was Maritime middleweight champion. Hardly a major title, but a title nonetheless. During this period he shifted his base from Cape Breton, where he had been associated with veteran promoter Gussie MacLellan, to Halifax, where he was welcomed by promoter Clary Harris, a local businessman.

Although he scored 20 knockouts in his first 25 fights, his technique was still unrefined. Better training and better sparring partners were required. So while MacLellan and Harris competed for his allegiance, in 1960 Richardson slipped away to Boston where he sought out Fat Johnny Buckley, then in his 70s. It was an odd pairing. Buckley was bitter, crude, opinionated and mob-connected. But for Richardson's boxing desires he was exquisite. Few knew the sport as well as Fat Johnny.

While he trained and lived in Boston, Richardson still fought in the Maritimes for MacLellan and Harris. In the early 1960s, when an average young man earned $2,000 a year, Richardson was harvesting $3,000 to $6,000 a match. By comparison, most undercard fighters pocketed just $200. "Nobody ever put a figure on it," Leland Richardson observed, "but I remember one time I heard him say — I guess when he was 16 or 17 — that he could have bought any car he wanted."

He was worth the price of a ticket. His matches were spellbinding.

In 1960 he was felled by local journeyman Al Rose at the opening bell. His vision blurred and his jaw broken, he fought on, barely able to open his mouth wide enough to spit out the blood. In the fifth round he broke his hand. But just one round later he caught Rose with a right cross and knocked him out. "They could count me out or carry me out," Richardson explained after the bout. "A lot of people paid to see that fight and I didn't want to disappoint them." The next day a surgeon wired Richardson's jaw. The fighter ate through a straw for two months.

He lost a 10-round decision in 1963 to Joey Archer, the world's second-ranked middleweight, in Madison Square Garden — the first Cape Bretoner to fight at what was still the sport's most prestigious address. "He hit me harder than I've ever been hit," observed Archer, who had fought almost all of the top middleweights of the era.

Richardson fought Burke Emery, from Sherbrooke, Quebec,

three times. Emery was Canadian light heavyweight champion in 1961 when they first met, before 6,000 spectators — the largest Halifax fight crowd to that point. Early in the contest Richardson fractured his right hand, but by the middle rounds he had opened three cuts on Emery's face and closed one of his eyes. However, late in the fight Emery landed two right hooks to the chin. Richardson crumpled to the canvas, where he was counted out. Hundreds of spectators left their seats and quietly encircled the ring. Three months later Richardson won their non-title rematch on a decision, after which Emery departed Halifax with his arm in a sling and his face a patchwork of magenta welts. Richardson won their third match, in mid-1962, again on a decision.

Ninth-ranked Joe DeNucci, a Boston streetfighter, faced Richardson twice in Glace Bay. In the first fight, 5,000 spectators winced as DeNucci landed one low blow after another. Richardson refused to reciprocate. "I just couldn't do it," he explained. DeNucci was disqualified, snarling that his young opponent had actually quit.

Before their rematch Richardson warned DeNucci that he would retaliate in kind if DeNucci again struck him with low blows. Undeterred, early in the fight DeNucci promptly smashed him in the groin. The response was pitiless. Richardson planted two stiff shots into DeNucci's crotch, opened cuts above DeNucci's eyes, sent him through the ropes twice, knocked him down once, and pounded his face into a puffy, grotesque mask. Years later DeNucci, who in the early 1970s was elected Massachusetts state auditor, called Richardson "a credit to boxing and to Canada."

Richardson's station in Maritime sports folklore became permanent after his three battles in the early 1960s with an Albertan named Wilfie Greaves. "The three most savage wars that I had ever seen in my life," states Pat Connolly, who described all three over a network of Maritime radio stations.

Managed by a wealthy industrialist from Detroit, Greaves ran two miles each day and downed high-protein beverages. He neither drank nor smoked. Save for a nose flattened by a head butt, Greaves' face bore no hint of his trade or technique. This was remarkable because Wilfie Greaves loved to brawl and didn't give a damn with whom. At mid-career no Canadian fighter of his generation had faced such formidable competition — Gene Fulmer, Tiger Jones, Spider Webb, Joey Giardello, Dick Tiger, Sugar Ray Robinson — top-line Americans against whom Greaves usually lost, but never without getting in his licks. He had more success in Canada. He won the Canadian middleweight championship in 1958, but two years later still had not defended the title. He claimed to have had trouble finding respectable opponents.

He found one in Blair Richardson.

The first of their three fights was Richardson's initial bid for a national title. Working in Greaves' corner was Tom McCluskey, a trainer from Halifax. It would be the only time that McCluskey worked opposite Richardson, and his presence was a paramount advantage for Greaves.

A day or so before the fight, McCluskey travelled to Glace Bay at the bidding of Clary Harris, who was struggling with Gussie MacLellan for control over Richardson. It would help Harris if Richardson did poorly on a MacLellan card.

McCluskey found Greaves on a bed in a hotel room downtown. His trainer was stretched out on the other bed. McCluskey stood in the doorway and introduced himself. The fighter grunted. McCluskey bristled. "Jesus, you fellas think you're on a picnic down here or somethin', don't ya?"

Greaves looked up. "Whatya mean?"

"You know what you're up against here?" asked McCluskey, his voice rising. "Do you *know* what this is all about? Have you *any idea* what's takin' place?"

"Well," said Greaves, "I'm fightin' this guy from Cape Breton."

"Cape Breton? *Cape Breton?* Jesus, this is where he was *born*, but he trains in *Boston*." Greaves raised his head a couple of inches. McCluskey continued. "Do you know how hard Blair Richardson hits?"

"Don't care," Greaves sneered. "What's your point?"

"Who sent you here?" asked Greaves' trainer.

"Harris," said McCluskey. Greaves reclined, pronouncing his interests secure with Gussie MacLellan.

"Gussie's a hit man!" shouted McCluskey. "Gussie's a henchman! Gussie wants you guys crucified! Gussie wants Wilfie taken out of here on a stretcher!"

Greaves' eyes widened. McCluskey lowered his voice and spread his arms. "You want me to stay or you want me to go?"

"Sit down," said Wilfie Greaves. "Fill me in."

The Richardson–Greaves series commenced in July 1962 in the Glace Bay Forum before a capacity crowd of 4,600, amid dense cigarette smoke and 100-degree heat. A few open windows and doors provided the only ventilation. Richardson began well, but in the middle rounds Greaves seized the fight. In the 10th round he swarmed and hooked, belting Richardson halfway through the ropes and hovering over him as he slumped in a neutral corner. Twice Greaves motioned to the referee to stop the fight. When he finally did, Richardson went directly to the local hospital where he was treated overnight for exhaustion.

In a car returning to Halifax after the fight, Greaves leaned from the back seat and placed a hand on McCluskey's shoulder. "If you hadn't levelled with me, he'd have killed me tonight." McCluskey shrugged. Greaves then reached into his pocket and pulled out $200. "Take this."

"I don't want it," said McCluskey, "I'm being paid by the promoter."

"Take it!" demanded Greaves.

"Thanks," said McCluskey.

McCluskey was not at Greaves' side when he lost the Canadian middleweight title to Richardson in their second fight, two months later, also in Glace Bay. In Richardson's corner was the ill-tempered but shrewd Fat Johnny Buckley.

During the fight Richardson applied crisp left jabs to stave off Greaves, flattening the Albertan's nose and opening a wide gash under his right eye. In the eighth round Richardson stormed from his corner and smashed an array of rights to Greaves' head as hundreds of patrons dashed to the edge of the ring. Greaves tumbled. His handlers quickly stopped the fight.

Their final contest unfolded at a sold-out, stultifying Halifax

Forum in May 1963. Richardson started magnificently, but Greaves came back in the later rounds with a blizzard of lefts and rights originating from all heights and angles. Richardson ended the fight bleeding, glassy-eyed and tangled in the ropes. He awaited the decision in his corner, dazed, propped on his stool, his rib cage an ugly mass of red blotches from the many body blows. Moments after Richardson was announced the winner — by unanimous decision — his seconds assisted him to his feet, then, like puppeteers, raised his limp arms to acknowledge the cheering. "Bleary-eyed Blair," the *Edmonton Journal* chided.

The next day he was admitted to Halifax's Victoria General Hospital. Brain damage was rumoured, but no such injury was found. "Blair is perfectly well," a hospital spokesman said. "He's getting masses of visitors. He's recovered very quickly." Nevertheless, doctors held him an extra day for observation.

Beverly Richardson later recalled that the inner voice commanding her husband to retire had resonated well before the warfare with Wilfie Greaves. "He got the message from the Lord: 'That's enough, fella.' "

Boxing had been overtaken by religion and an array of related interests including youth work. "Blair Richardson read his Bible every evening before he went in the ring," says Tom McCluskey. "He never liked that there be cursin'. He never liked any bad talk. He was a holy man."

Richardson's religious conversion began one evening in 1960 in Bar Harbor, Maine, where he had gone to rest after a fight. There, on a beach, he was introduced to 35-year-old Reverend John DeBrine. DeBrine was pastor at Boston's Ruggles Street Baptist Church and a radio evangelist whose religious program, *Songtime*, was heard on nearly 200 stations in the United States. The pair chatted.

Richardson tentatively accepted DeBrine's invitation to attend one of his services. "I used to go to church at Christmas and Easter, weather permitting, but that was about it," the fighter later admitted.

True to his word, one Sunday morning Richardson ascended the steps of Ruggles Street Baptist, near downtown Boston, accompanied by a couple of chums from the gym whom he persuaded to come along for support. The trio settled into a pew near the back.

At some point during the service 21-year-old Richardson rose, approached the altar and knelt. "Oh Jesus," he said, his eyes tightly shut. "I invite you to come and live in my spirit."

Back in the pews one of his buddies smiled. "He's got religion," he whispered.

Richardson later declared that moment "changed my whole outlook." It certainly established a friendship. The pugilist and the pastor, both bachelors at the time, became close friends and eventually roommates. Although he would not officially retire for several years, Richardson's path away from the ring was now assured.

Also during this period he enrolled at Boston's Emerson College, a small non-denominational institution known for its speech department — and the disproportionate success of its graduates in politics and the media. Early semesters were tough for a young man with a fragile academic disposition. At least one Emerson professor could not even understand him through his Cape Breton accent. But others saw his potential.

"I recognized in Blair something that was very real and earnest and good, all of it hidden under a very rough exterior," Kenneth Crannell, head of the speech department, told *Weekend Magazine*. "I never had a student who developed so quickly over such a relatively short time. In the beginning, though, it was difficult. I was always trying to get him out of himself. I used to call him 'animal' — just to try and get some sort of reaction out of him. This went on for I don't know how long, but one day it had its effect. One day, after I'd called him animal his fists started to clench, and I said, 'Go on, hit me! Go ahead and hit me!' That was the breaking point. After that I got through to him and in terms of learning he became the proverbial sponge."

By his retirement from boxing in 1967 Richardson was pursuing a master's degree in communication and was working as a teaching assistant at Emerson. He took to the campus stage to read Thurber, cummings, Frost and Browning. He even helped host DeBrine's radio show. Prizefighting offered no comparable fulfilment. "His boxing career ended not in failure, but in boredom," a close friend from Boston reflected. "Just before his last scheduled fight he told me, 'I couldn't care less.' "

His final two fights testified to his mindset, falling well short of a classic *denouement*. In June 1966 he scored a lacklustre technical knockout in Saint John, New Brunswick, against a puffed-up welterweight, Paul Christie. A month later he fought New Yorker Isaac Logart to a draw in Halifax. Fans jeered throughout and greeted the decision with catcalls. "[There] was not a single highlight in the 10 rounds," wrote veteran *Chronicle-Herald* columnist Ace Foley. "[You'd] expect a man rated in the top 10 to be able to get something going and Richardson's image was tarnished mainly because he didn't throw enough punches."

A few months after the Logart fight, Richardson signed to defend his Canadian title in Glace Bay against Jimmy Meilleur, a 26-year-old Canadian Press teletype operator. The match never took place, much to the disappointment of Meilleur and his team.

In Moncton, New Brunswick, a week after Richardson announced his retirement, the president of the Canadian Professional Boxing Federation stressed that the championship would not merely be flipped arbitrarily to a convenient suitor. "They're going to have to fight for it," proclaimed Sam Ermen Sr.

And who would *they* be? he was asked.

"Jimmy Meilleur."

And who else?

"The next person in line."

Meaning who?

"I can't say right offhand," said Ermen.

In North End Halifax, where he and his common-law wife were raising their four children, David Downey looked on as another year of empty aspiration wafted past. In the summer of Canada's centennial his boxing career was dormant, and many questioned his commitment to the sport.

At age 25, a prizefighter's prime, Downey owned a novice's resume: seven wins and one loss in seven years. Halifax's fight scene had slowed, and overtures — at least ones Downey found reasonable — were few. Thirteen months since his last fight he had receded from public consciousness, his life now drawn to his children and his labour job with the provincial government.

He still ventured to city gyms, but once there found earnest effort increasingly difficult to summon. His so-called management team appeared comatose. Local sportswriters thought him retired. Officials at the Canadian Professional Boxing Federation did not even consider him when first scheduling a series of matches to determine Richardson's successor.

The federation proposed a tournament pitting number-one-ranked Meilleur against Montreal's Leonardo Ianna, and Vancouver's Jim Walters against Brantford, Ontario's Gary Broughton. The winners would then contest for the Canadian middleweight championship.

But providence — and poverty — would play their part.

"Canadian boxing officials decided against an elimination runoff due to geographical difficulties," reported the *Chronicle-Herald* late that summer, covering for the fact that the participants were too broke to travel. So the federation moved to Plan B: in essence, settle the matter quickly by locating someone — anyone — to face Jimmy Meilleur for the title. Scrolling an inventory of possible opponents, conjecturing that interest in the fight was likely highest in Halifax, officials came to Downey's name.

Sound win-loss record. Hometown boy. No travel costs. That he had not fought in more than a year apparently mattered little.

Downey learned of his good fortune from his trainer Vince Hennebury one evening after a light workout at the Creighton Street Gym. "David, we got the break of our lives!" announced Hennebury, his hand squeezing his fighter's shoulder. "You know what? You can beat him!"

Plucked from obscurity like a Bluenose version of Rocky Balboa, the quirky, despondent fictional character from the movie *Rocky,* Downey immediately sensed he was finally about to rise into the higher stratum of local fighters such as Richardson and lightweight Kid Howard. That night he was too excited to sleep. "I was trying to picture in my mind, me entering the ring and everybody there, full, from Halifax, seein' me, from here, Creighton Street. Gonna be the top fight on the card. I was gonna be the big cheese!"

Downey's giddy anticipation blinded him to one obvious fact: Halifax in the 1960s had only one desired complexion for a big cheese. And it was not his.

The black population across Nova Scotia was hopelessly under-represented in every hall of power and influence — business, academia and politics. While through the decades several Nova Scotian black fighters were admired, they did not incite the civic passion of Richardson or Howard, both white in a blood sport shamelessly seeking Great White Hopes and exploiting ethnic division. During calm periods the transition from a popular white champion to a black champion would have been a thorny issue. In the heated 1960s, it carried even more baggage.

But this did not impede Downey's enthusiasm as he trained for Meilleur in Boston, the American city that for generations has possessed a persistent and almost mystical draw for Maritimers, athletes included. There, in a downtown gym, Downey found Fat Johnny Buckley — mystical in his own right — who had previously counselled Blair Richardson. Richardson also helped, his fee paid by Halifax businessman Victor Beed.

Downey and Richardson were never especially close. They would encounter one another at the Halifax Forum or in a local gym and the interaction would be courteous, but always superficial and brief. Around Richardson, Downey felt like an interloper.

"The people made him like he was untouchable," says Downey. "[Even when he retired] they were not going to let go of him because he was the Golden Boy. He came from Cape Breton and there's a lot of Cape Bretoners in Halifax. And they loved him."

Richardson's handlers once barred Downey from his dressing room when Downey merely wanted to wish Richardson well before a fight. The snub was never forgotten. "I said, 'the hell with it! Frig 'em! When my time comes around, I'll be like that when some of them come to me.'

"Blair was a loner. Me, I like to be around a lot of people. At the weigh-in they used to keep him alone. I used to come out and talk to people. He never did that. I think they sheltered him too much. Because you have to be able to mingle with people. If you bottle things up it may make you worry about things. I think, 'It's another fight, it's another day.' He probably wasn't getting the joy out of it. I got the joy out of it."

In Boston, however, near the end of Downey's training, the two shared at least one private moment.

"David, I don't need to tell you anything, really," Richardson said. "You're good. Very good. I thought you and me were going to have to fight someday."

Downey nodded. "I thought the same thing."

"I truthfully believe you're gonna win this title. And I hate to say this, but you know how things are back home."

"What ya mean?"

"Well, you're probably not going to be treated like I am."

Today Downey recalls those comments and shrugs. "I think he was referring to the race thing. And he meant that I was never, never gonna get the money he was getting.

"And he was right."

2

BOILING

Jimmy Meilleur's pugilistic virtues began and ended with toughness. But even with limited skills, Meilleur was confident he could defeat Downey and finally secure the title he had felt imminent when Blair Richardson left him at the altar earlier in the year.

Meilleur was an inch taller than Downey and owned a heftier frame. He was also more experienced. Meilleur had 15 fights — six wins, seven losses, two draws — compared with Downey's eight, none scheduled for more than eight rounds. Most importantly, Meilleur had been active recently. Only seven weeks earlier he had lost a strenuous 12-round decision to Jamaican Milo Calhoun for the vacant British Empire title.

The Halifax media warmed to a Downey-Meilleur bout, just as the Canadian Professional Boxing Federation had calculated. Local sportswriters eagerly cast the match as the enigmatic Downey's reckoning. Wrote *Chronicle-Herald* sports editor Ace Foley, "David Downey has been clamouring for recognition as a topflight boxer for some years and as a preliminary fighter showed considerable promise. He hasn't been very active, but he has been insisting he belongs with the best in Canada."

The fight was promoted by Halifax Raceway Limited, a fledgling sports concern led by local businessmen Victor Beed and Fred Lahey. Halifax Raceway ostensibly aimed to construct — with taxpayers' help — a premium boxing gymnasium in the North End. It also had designs on a winter horse-racing franchise and pro wrestling promotion. But mainly it sought to revitalize prize-fighting in the city. Indeed, Downey-Meilleur headlined the first professional boxing event in more than a year at the Halifax Forum, a site unaccustomed to such a lengthy calm.

The hallowed Halifax Forum was in decay. It had opened in 1926 — on Boxing Day, appropriately. No activity or sport through the years would be more apt for this sprawling brick structure in the city's middle-class west end. Boxing and the building shared a propensity to endure despite periodic fervent opinion they should not.

Talk of demolishing the Forum was rife around the period of Downey-Meilleur. Developers from across the region were proposing multi-million dollar visions for the site. One of the more lavish emanated from a young Saint John, New Brunswick, developer named Pat Rocca, who suggested a $75-million complex that included an 800-room hotel, an 18,000-seat arena, a 45,000-seat football stadium and an underground parking garage for 5,000 cars.

"The current Forum building is old, small — in spots unclean and all the paint jobs in the world cannot hide the usage or wear and tear that years have brought it," wrote broadcaster Alex J. Walling in the *Scotian Journalist*. "[It's] outdated and dying a disturbing death [and] no longer is respected, being described as a 'barn,' 'dungeon' or 'pit.' "

But grand schemes foundered, and broad disdain gradually evaporated like the smoky haze on fight night. And the Forum survived more or less intact, according to broadcaster Pat Connolly, "for reasons more emotional than practical."

To reach the Forum, patrons hiked across a small parking lot to a slightly sunken main entrance displaying a row of narrow wooden doors. Inside, the scent of sweat and must fused with odours of french fries, hot dogs, cigars, hair oil, booze, salt air, cheap perfume and car exhaust. All were absorbed into walls regularly slathered with oil-based paint, which itself added a chemical twist to the aroma. During fight cards, cigarette smoke formed a haze so dense it obscured the ring for spectators as close as 15 rows back.

The Forum held 5,500 or so for hockey, and about 6,500 for

boxing, when folding chairs were placed 20 rows deep around the ring. The building's south end had no elevated seats, but was brightened for generations by an analogue hockey clock presenting the porcelain countenance of the Macdonald Exports cigarette girl.

On boxing nights most reporters sat ringside. Those who didn't proceeded upstairs to a couple of old press boxes, precariously suspended mere feet above the heads of spectators. CBC television's boxing voice of the 1970s and 1980s, Doug Saunders, grimaces at the thought of those boxes. "Christ, you took your life in your hands on the catwalk trying to get out to them. The Forum [was] always, always, always, always dirty. There were cigarette butts in the urinals. The pillars in the place blocked your view. But the place just reeks of atmosphere. I just love the Halifax Forum."

"When I look back at my career here," reflects sportscaster and newsman Harris Sullivan, "the Forum almost becomes the first thing I think of — not the legislature, not the television station where I spent 22 years. It was the same sort of feeling that people have who were associated with Maple Leaf Gardens or the Montreal Forum."

The fighters used hockey dressing rooms that featured a mirror, a couple of sinks, a urinal or two, three showerheads and an open toilet. Wooden benches lined the walls. Security was scarce, so hangers-on of both genders had easy access. "I always think it was a good thing for a manager [to] put the fighter's name on one door, [then] move him to another room," says Halifax promoter Sonny MacPhee. "We always used to find something small — like something the doctor was going to use for an examining room before the fights — and use that."

On September 18, 1967, Jimmy Meilleur and a couple of cornermen entered the Forum ring minutes ahead of Downey, who arrived with a troop worthy of a conquistador. Almost a dozen strong and emerging from the east, Downey's supporters — including Blair Richardson — advanced down a wide passage lined with steel chairs and half-familiar faces. The voices of trainer Vince Hennebury and manager Murray Langford merged with the shouts of relatives and friends sucked into a moment of hometown celebrity. About 2,500 patrons rose and turned to glimpse the hooded figure in a red, crushed-velvet robe trimmed in gold. On the back of the robe, high and centred, in gold, was stitched *Dave Downey*.

Dance up the steps … dip between the ropes … spring into the ring … celebrate with raised hands and a blizzard of punches — one-two-three-four-five-six-seven-eight-nine — punches too fast for the untrained eye to count … hear the crowd cheer and hoot, acknowledging that in the ring now stands *a big cheese*.

At the bell Downey's aggression and fast hands surprised Meilleur, who seemed a half-beat behind. The local fighter moved fluidly, landing swift combinations then stepping back to hunt for a point of entry for another flurry. But by the later rounds Downey's pace — risky for a fighter inexperienced in long matches — caused him to tire. In the ninth, Meilleur "came in and threw that wild swing at me, and he did catch me and sort of knocked me down — I was off balance. I got up and I said [to myself], 'You'll never put that punch on me again.' And then I just played a tune with him."

In the 11th and 12th rounds Downey cracked rapid combinations to Meilleur's head and body, then taunted him by keeping his hands at his side, tempting the larger man to charge forward and open himself to counterpunches. Meilleur did not take the bait.

"He did dirty tricks," says Downey. "He used his elbows, [he tried] to hold me in the corner and hit me. He couldn't catch me [so] he tried to tackle me like a football player and put me in the corner."

"Meilleur had the opportunity more than anybody else to take Dave out with one shot," says Sonny MacPhee, who was present that night. "I think he knew that he could and planned on doin' it. A couple of times he hit Dave and it jarred him because you could tell with the little jiggle in his step. A couple of times when he went back to the corner he wasn't what he should be, but Dave had the ability to rise to the occasion."

Downey won by unanimous decision. Moments after the announcement, at ring centre, in a ceremony that underlined the importance of boxing to civic pride, North End alderman

Walter Fitzgerald handed him the ornate belt of the Canadian middleweight champion.

Except it was not *really* the ornate belt of the Canadian middleweight champion. The Canadian Professional Boxing Federation couldn't find the actual belt. So in a panic a day or so before the fight someone contacted *The Ring* magazine and borrowed a belt from Sandy Saddler, the retired world featherweight championship. No one in the crowd noticed the ruse. And the new champion didn't seem to care much.

At the time.

But the *faux* belt has since taken on deeper significance.

"That's a slap in the face to me, like a lot of slaps in the face," says Downey. Despite holding the middleweight title for many years, and despite several requests, he never received the authentic championship belt. "That shows you that the Canadian Boxing Federation didn't have decency enough with the fighters. I never even had a chance to get a picture with it on. They didn't respect me."

Torso glistening, Downey stood in his dressing room as family, friends and smiling faces he did not recognize squeezed in to share his rapture. "Champion," he whispered to himself, his eyes moist. "Canadian champion."

"[It] has been a quick jump from obscurity to the top," wrote Ace Foley the next day. "Dave hasn't fought much in the past five years but perhaps winning the title will spur him on to activity in the months ahead. The Meilleur bout was the first time Downey went past six rounds in a fight so he has a lot to learn, but he appears to be enthusiastic, showed superb physical condition, commendable speed and courage in getting up off the floor to win."

Downey departed the Forum in his brother Billy's metallic gold Cadillac De Ville — a gift from local developer Ralph Medjuck — destined for the Carleton Hotel, owned by Victor Beed. A large buffet was set out in the lobby, now teeming with many of the city's most affluent businessmen and well-known politicians. Blair Richardson stood off in a corner. When Downey beckoned him closer Richardson moved past quickly. "David, it's your night, not mine," he said.

Downey worked the crowd and smiled for a half-hour. He then took a telephone call. "David, the band's playin'!" his brother Billy screamed into the receiver from his North End nightspot, the Arrows Club. "Everybody's here. They're waiting for *you.*"

The new champion headed for the Arrows, leaving a mostly white gathering for one that was mostly black, innocently and elegantly knitting the demographics of a racially tense city.

"You couldn't believe the entrée when I walked through that door," remembers Downey, his eyes welling up with the recollection. "They stood up, everybody in the place. I was crying and everything because of the joy, the happiness. Everybody come and hugged me — my father was sitting there and I ran right over and hugged him. The guys in the band called me up because my brother Billy wanted to introduce me to all the people. Then when I got off the stage I never saw so many women coming up and hugging me and lookin' at me. I never did sleep that night."

He remained at the Arrows until close to 4 am, then repaired to a friend's house where he stayed until around 7 am, when he strolled down to Gottingen Street, the neighbourhood's commercial and entertainment heart.

The news had already reached the streets.

"All the stores were opening up, and all the people kept comin' out on Gottingen Street. I went to the meat market that I always dealt with. I went to order a roast and they gave me a roast *and* a big steak, three inches thick [that] would have fed two or three people. They said, 'This roast can be for the rest of the family, but this is yours — a champion steak!' "

While the North End celebrated Downey's triumph, the rest of the city was much less excited — just one symptom of a simmering racial divide that was about to erupt.

"There is a problem," proclaimed Jules Oliver, a young black man appointed in the late 1960s by Halifax mayor Allan O'Brien to investigate unfair employment practices in the city. "A problem that can be summed up in two words — social injustice. No matter how desperately one seeks to deny it, this simple fact persists and intrudes itself. It is the fuel of protests and revolts."

The fuel had fomented quietly for generations, unseen by white Nova Scotians programmed to understand unemployment and poverty as simply the lot of the coloureds, and unchallenged by black Nova Scotians tolerant of their subordinate position in society. According to Donald Oliver, a relative of Jules and himself a young activist Halifax lawyer at the time, racism was a fact of life for black Nova Scotians, comparable to Mississippi and Alabama where basic human rights and services were routinely denied.

The list of indignities seemed as long and as wide as the province itself.

In Halifax and Dartmouth during the period after the Second World War, blacks were commonly refused service in restaurants, hotels and barber shops. Many lived in deplorable housing — some rural communities had neither electric power nor flush toilets. Schools and churches were segregated. Movie theatres relegated black patrons to 'Nigger Heaven,' in the balcony. Black women were not allowed to train as nurses in Nova Scotia hospitals.

In Beechville, a poor black district west of Halifax, a black graduate student was offered work as a domestic by a white woman from the city who had randomly dialled a number in the Beechville exchange. She assumed that whoever answered would need a job.

In Digby, a 43-year-old black man was imprisoned for five months for being $80 in arrears on a poll tax.

In St. Croix, a black family was refused a permit to bury their three-year-old daughter at a cemetery where a 60-year-old bylaw barred "Negroes and Indians."

In Africville, a small black community on the shores of Bedford Basin, the city through the years had placed a dump and other facilities unwanted elsewhere in Halifax. It also withheld basic household services like running water. Having rendered the area virtually uninhabitable, and buoyed by the prevailing notion of slum clearance, local authorities expropriated the land in the early 1960s and began demolishing houses. Residents were scattered, many relocating to a large public housing complex in the North

End called Mulgrave Park. By the late 1960s Africville was a park. It has since become a searing public symbol of the government's callous treatment of blacks.

In the 1960s, with civil rights a conspicuous and broadening story in the United States, other parts of Canada suddenly grew curious about their own cultural currents and focused on Nova Scotia, which at the time was home to 15,000 of the 38,000 blacks in Canada.

"In the 40 blocks just north of Citadel Hill, dingy clapboard tenements house most of the city's 10,000 Negroes," wrote *Maclean's*. "Here, racial tension and poverty are the way of life. Large families of Negroes are commonly jammed into two or three rooms. Negro teenagers and young adults, whose main resting place is the dimly lit streets in the neighbourhood, are regularly passed by white police officers, dutifully enforcing laws against rowdyism and loitering."

Now and then, agreeable events such as David Downey's boxing achievement smoothed the jagged tenor of life in North End Halifax. But these were temporary distractions and had little lasting affect. "The ranks of the malcontents are swelling, racial tensions are on the increase and it's only a matter of time before the violence in the United States spills into Canada and the Maritimes," wrote Gus Wedderburn, president of the Nova Scotia Association for the Advancement of Coloured People.

If poverty was the foremost issue facing black Nova Scotians, the problem of leadership within their own community was not far behind. Wedderburn, from Jamaica, was typical of black leaders in that he was not Nova Scotia born and educated. In *Forgotten Canadians: The Blacks of Nova Scotia*, author Frances Henry wrote that for many years only a handful of people — notably members of the Oliver family — had taken on the role of community leadership. Henry noted that in the early 1960s black spokesmen in the province were often recent West Indian immigrants. "It is revealing of the level of oppression in the local community that leadership fell upon those who were foreign-born and trained."

Lacking a distinct philosophy or single leader around whom

they could coalesce, Nova Scotia blacks in 1967 disagreed over how to address their plight. A sizeable number favoured working from within, building a power base, first economically, then politically. Spokesmen for this approach were conventional, cautious men, usually well-educated. Many already held official posts in established government-funded organizations or smaller charities that survived mainly through public donations, mostly from whites.

While this reassured whites, a growing army of young blacks opposed the marriage of black progress to white largesse. For some, established bodies such as the Nova Scotia Association for the Advancement of Coloured People (NSAACP) were anachronisms, and their leaders were men without the personal voltage to charge a people or forge rapid change.

The movement, the *cause* — while served heroically over decades by a small knot of dedicated women and men — craved fresh representation and other strong voices.

In the late 1960s, for blacks in Halifax, two such voices spoke with remarkable clarity. Each offered inspiration, energy and credibility. One belonged to a moderate, the other to a militant. One restive pre-dawn morning in 1967 they would both be heard.

Some blacks believed that Delmore 'Buddy' Daye, 37, chairman of the NSAACP human rights committee, lived in whitey's side pocket. Some whites thought him a little man obsessed by race. The great mass in between regarded him as a paragon of forbearance. "Whatever Buddy could do to make a person a better human being, I think he did," says Alex J. Walling. "I called him Mr. Daye."

Born in New Glasgow in 1929, Daye was four years old when he and three brothers were sent to Halifax to live with their aunt after a family breakup. He grew up on Gottingen Street, where he introduced himself to the neighbourhood with the words, "Any of you guys wanna fight?"

As a child he was once physically thrown out of school for refusing to stand and read from the absurdly stereotypic book *The Adventures of Little Black Sambo*. "[My aunt] taught us that we weren't inferior to anyone, that we should not let anyone tell us that we were inferior, and not to act inferior," he later explained.

His adult life was rich, diverse and often dangerous. As a member of the merchant marine during the Second World War, he and his crewmates were placed in custody at a port in South Africa. At other points in his life Daye was a social worker, a railroad employee, a laundry manager, a political candidate, the sergeant-at-arms of the Nova Scotia House of Assembly and a boxing champion.

In the 1950s he held the Canadian junior lightweight title for a year and a half, and Maritime featherweight championship for five years. In total he won 81 matches and lost six, knocking out 71 opponents. Despite this success he never especially enjoyed the sport. "I didn't feel good when I lost, and I didn't feel good when I won. I was just trying to make a living, provide for my family."

By the late 1960s Daye was a force for black equality. He was involved in almost every issue of consequence for his community, including battles to hire black firemen, bus drivers and police officers — in a police force of 190 members, not one was black. He also lobbied to provide children with better access to recreational facilities. "Buddy was wise enough and smart enough to know who you had to do business with to get things done," says Pat Connolly. "And he put his neck on the line."

The other strong black voice belonged to Burnley 'Rocky' Jones, 26. No other Canadian better fit the prototype of '60s black militant. "I would give the inspiration of [Halifax's black] movement exclusively to Burnley Jones," reflects his activist partner and ex-wife Joan Jones. "He inspired people in a lot of ways."

"He was a *very* charismatic guy," says Harris Sullivan, who during the period was in the vanguard of white journalists delving into Nova Scotia's politics of race.

Rocky Jones was born in 1941 in Truro, Nova Scotia, about 60 miles north of Halifax, and raised in a small black community on the outskirts of town called The Marsh. He was the fourth of 10 children. "I was always the one in the family to fuck up," he once told the *Halifax Daily News*. While he did not fully comprehend it as a child, Jones was subject to racism in Truro only slightly less extreme than that of the American South. He was not allowed to bowl with whites at the local bowling alley (although he had a part-time job there). He could neither play at the local pool hall, nor eat in certain restaurants around town. He had white friends but was seldom invited to their parties.

"I knew that town would destroy me," he later reflected. While the local black community and his family gave him pride and purpose, "the town didn't give me shit." He joined the military reserves at age 13, then enlisted in the regular army through a special apprentice program. He was released about a year later. "I got into too much trouble."

In 1959 in Toronto he drove a tractor-trailer for a while, then got a job with the Ontario government treasury department where he worked with unit record machines, forerunners to the modern computer. His profound political awakening began there when he met and married Joan, his first wife, whose commitment to equality was by then well developed. White kids growing up in nearby Oakville, Ontario, learned the hard way that Joan accepted no guff and could make her point with her fists. "If somebody called me nigger — bang! I wasn't very big, but I was tough."

In Toronto, stimulating discussions were like oxygen to Jones, and he inhaled deeply. At home with Joan, on his job at the provincial treasury, through his university courses, in Village coffee shops listening to folksingers, "my consciousness-raising happened. It was like an explosion in your head. I just had a chance to learn-learn-learn-learn."

In 1965 he went to the United States, with the Student Union for Peace Action.

His public image developed suddenly, after a *Toronto Star* article on an anti-U.S. racism demonstration downtown dubbed him Canada's own Stokely Carmichael. "And I didn't know shit from shinnola," laughs Jones. "The press in Canada wanted to have a black militant that they could relate to. And I filled the bill."

On his return to Halifax, the impatient crusader among other activities founded the Kwacha (Freedom) Club, a group of 50 or so blacks, roughly aged 15 to 25, to which he taught his philosophy of social reform. Reported *Maclean's*, "The club's sessions aren't always orderly, and its dances run loud and late. As a result, the club has just been kicked out of its third premises in three years."

Around the city and throughout the province Jones — resplendent with his traditional African clothing, his Vandyke like Malcolm X's — gave impassioned speeches with dire undertones. With one glare through his large dark-rimmed glasses he terrified half the whites in Halifax. Certainly the authorities took him seriously.

The national press could not resist him either. Jones brilliantly turned this attention to his advantage by exploiting a fundamentally unsophisticated media to deliver his messages and help alter the national consciousness.

In a classic piece of '60s' reportage entitled 'Rocky The Revolutionary,' *Globe and Mail* writer Martin O'Malley dutifully noted the presence of guns and anger in Jones' home. At one point O'Malley described Jones as he read aloud one of his old speeches. "You whites who merely mouth the words of sympathy, understanding the desire for us to wait just a little longer rank no higher in my estimation than the white bastards who so very methodically put the bullets through the heads of our young black children. There is much to be done, but the door of freedom has been thrown open wide. I'm going to sing — no! I'm going to shout, I'm going to demand, freedom now!"

Former Halifax mayor Walter Fitzgerald knew both Daye and Jones well. "Totally different. Different size, different personality, different objective. Rocky was a very tall, outgoing individual. He was very influential and very straightforward. He was a leader and very vocal, and perhaps he did scare a few people. Rocky probably scared people more than Buddy."

Rocky Jones agrees the images contrasted. "We were up and down, me and Buddy," he reflects. "The establishment couldn't use me for anything because they didn't trust me. I could never be *inside*, and they couldn't control me because I didn't care about money [and] I couldn't be physically intimidated. But for Buddy, he had a large family and he didn't have much education. He didn't have many options and he had to play the game. He didn't have any choices. I had lots of choices. This was a big difference [between us]."

Another difference was tactics. Jones, who once mused with others about establishing a commando training camp in Nova Scotia, says his side sought to expose "the yin and the yang," accentuating the contrasts. "We had this saying, 'You've got to heighten the contradictions. You must have a confrontation. And out of that you can have resolution. But without the contradictions and the confrontation there is no resolution.' Buddy was very much interested in the compromise and avoiding the confrontation."

On Thursday, August 31, 1967, Haligonians awoke to the headline: 'Africville to be Demolished.' Bulldozers were ready, the *Chronicle-Herald* reported, "to begin demolishing the last section of the Negro slum once described as an 'indictment of society.'" Good morning.

That night there was a rock 'n' roll dance at the Halifax Forum. Around midnight, shortly after it ended, a scuffle broke out in the parking lot. Most of those involved were black. Police arrived and arrested a large 17-year-old named Wayne Smith (who joined the Ottawa Rough Riders of the Canadian Football League a couple of years later and began a long career as an all-star defensive end).

Upset by the arrest, 40 or so black youths stormed off the Forum property and headed down Almon Street, their anger building. With cops following closely, the mob turned onto Agricola Street, then onto West Street where, according to *Maclean's*, they indiscriminately hurled bricks and bottles. One police officer was kicked and injured and a patrol car damaged. More cops arrived and made two more arrests. With the mood and the numbers escalating, the cops grew increasingly nervous.

Around this time police summoned Buddy Daye to try and calm the group. *Maclean's* reports that Daye drew off eight of the more belligerent members and took them back to his home on nearby Creighton Street, where he listened to their frustrations until 4 am.

Daye later told the magazine he took guns from two of them.

Rocky Jones offers a slightly different account. He says that the horde was about to turn on Daye, so cops sought him out. They had no trouble finding him. Jones was under constant surveillance, and they knew he was at a friend's house in another part of the city. They pounded on the door.

"We've got a problem," said a cop. "You've got to come and do somethin'. "

"What's the problem?" Jones asked.

"There's a riot."

They briefed Jones in a patrol car as it sped across town. He was strategically dropped off on Cunard Street, a block or so from the mob, which now numbered about 100 and had drifted down to the corner of Gottingen and Gerrish streets. Jones walked up to the youths, taking stock of the riot cops and other officers hidden in the shadows. "These cops were scared shitless. And here are the kids, they've got sticks and stones and these cops have guns. And I say to myself, '*Now what?*' Quite clearly, you couldn't defuse a situation like that by saying 'go home.' It would be absolutely impossible."

Jones turned to the youths.

"Look at these minions," he screamed, pointing to the police. "These fuckin' beat cops. Forget 'em! We've not talkin' to *them*. We're not dealing with *them*. Don't even bother with them. Leave these guys alone. They can't solve our problem. We are taking this to the police station."

"Those officers were literally trembling," reflects Jones today. "And these kids were not going to back off for nothin'. It was close. I just knew I had to get these kids out of there."

And so the trek began, six blocks down the middle of Gottingen Street, angry chants echoing off the shops and stores as startled drivers jerked their cars onto the sidewalks. It was now after 1 am.

At the end of their journey awaited a tall, gaunt, grim-faced 52-year-old named Verdun Mitchell, the chief of police. Mitchell stood erect on the steps of police headquarters, then located at the corner of Brunswick and Market streets. He was facing the harbour, looking down at the mob. At his back were a dozen heavily armed cops — all white.

Fellow officers considered Mitchell a progressive thinker and a man composed under pressure. Now, in the darkness, the enlightened administrator confronted Rocky Jones.

Jones gave Mitchell an ultimatum: release the black prisoners involved in the fight outside the Forum, or try to place the entire crowd under arrest. Mitchell coolly rejected both options. The two sides repeated variations of their positions for half an hour, while the mob shouted and the armed cops stared. Finally, Mitchell invited Jones and a couple of others into his office. Once inside Mitchell began with a statement: *Under no circumstances would the arrested kids be released.* "We didn't have a long discussion because he was very clear," recalls Jones.

Then, around 2 am, a compromise was struck. Mitchell said that everybody in the group could come into the station and talk to the arrested youths, who would remain in their cells. And so, two or three at a time, young black men walked up the steps into the station, past armed white cops, for a few minutes with the arrested youths. By dawn, everyone had left peacefully.

"I had so much time for Verdun Mitchell," says Jones today. "I think he was a great chief. Smart."

One of the few witnesses not directly involved in the incident was CJCH's Harris Sullivan, Halifax's quintessential young '60s liberal journalist. Sullivan came across the turmoil on his way home. His tape recorder was nearby. The happenstance would elevate his career and influence the debate on local race relations for years.

"It was a nothing event, a fight that turned into a big racial event. The only thing that saved it was Verdun Mitchell. It had the potential to be a terrible, terrible thing, and it was fairly serious for about an hour. Verdun Mitchell stayed up all night talking the thing down, them down. Keeping his cool. The cops were ready to come in and bang heads, that sort of thing."

Sullivan captured it all on tape, staying on the scene until 5 am. His five-minute report aired a few hours later and included parts of the talk-down by Mitchell. "I suddenly realized — never mind the scoop I got on it — with that incident we had potential problems here because of the hatred that was coming from the blacks, voiced in this minor, minor incident.

"I couldn't get over the depths of the anger. I became interested in the fact that this is not just potentially a very big story down the road, this is an important development in the history of the city. All of a sudden these black guys were no longer fighting the cops, they were sort of expressing something more than just animosity over whatever minor incident that started it. But there was so much electricity and dynamics involved. Even Verdun Mitchell cried. He recognized it, and he backed everybody off.

"It didn't really turn into a riot. It was the dynamics — the potential of it all — that scared the hell out of me. Up until then most people were of the opinion that Halifax was just a peaceful and co-operative model community involving the black community. Uh-huh. What this showed was there was a lot boiling under the surface."

The daily newspaper typically underplayed the incident. The next day the *Mail-Star* carried a four-inch story on the front page describing how "25–30 boys and girls arrived at the police station demanding to see their friends." Another three-inch report on page two listed the accused and their related minor charges. It gave few other details.

No mention was made of the race of the accused.

A few weeks later city council gave Buddy Daye a two-year appointment (annual salary $6,000) to serve as a youth organizer in the North End. Meanwhile, Rocky Jones continued to build a power base that would rivet attention on the black cause, demanding immediate action on such issues as housing reform and employment.

Maclean's wrote, "Who's likely to do more to avert the danger of race riots in Halifax — Rocky Jones, a Black Power advocate urging young Negroes to examine their relationship with white society, or Buddy Daye, a congenial moderate trying to distract them with volleyball and ping-pong and a lot of dandy games?"

3

LA DOLCE VITA

"The North End is a state of mind that cannot be defined in terms of geography," Halifax schoolteacher Terrence Punch once wrote. "It requires a conscious facing up to the fact that, all things being equal, North End students can go as far and do as well as any others. I have not said that success is easier or easy for North Enders; I do say that one of the obstacles in the way to success is a state of mind that claims inferiority for oneself on the grounds of being a North Ender."

A three-square-mile patch on the northeast corner of the Halifax peninsula, the North End slopes downward towards the harbour, as if to chart a life course for its underclass. The area is a melting pot, having through the years attracted Indians, Italians, Jews, Muslims, Russians, Germans and Asians, among others. Mostly, however, it has been the domain of working-class whites, whose ancestors arrived seeking a better life, and blacks, some of whose ancestors arrived in shackles.

The more fortunate members of successive generations found adequate jobs and serviceable homes off the main drag. The less successful of all races found themselves in public housing — clusters of subsidized, government-constructed boxes that for decades have incubated crime and restlessness.

"The groups in the upper part of the community didn't associate with the people down in the public housing," says Walter Fitzgerald, who in the 1960s taught school in the area. "[But residents] seemed to be proud they were North Enders. It was a real state. 'I'm from the North End,' and that was good. Everyone respected that."

The North End's temporal endowments are few and modest. Small businesses such as drug stores and pawnshops dominate. Most homes are either tiny bungalows or two-storey structures, many in gaudy colours, some having two or three add-ons. The area's nucleus is the Halifax Commons, a lazy, pastoral checkerboard of softball diamonds and assorted recreation enticements such as wading pools and tennis courts. A large fountain — a civic emblem of sorts — was erected in the '60s and used for years by a local TV station as the opening image for its movie of the week. In the warmer months, hookers plied their trade, concealed by randomly positioned bushes.

The central business concourse is Gottingen Street, which bisects the community geographically while stitching it together socially and economically. In the mid-1900s prosperous businesses bearing names such as Rubin's, Gene's Fish Market, Gordon B. Isnor's, Harnish's, Cline's and Sack's gave the street a distinct and respectable commercial identity that in latter years would be usurped by tawdry enterprises such as strip joints, massage parlours, crack houses, tattoo parlours, soft-core porn theatres and whorehouses.

The area also once included Africville, an eighteenth-century safe haven for African slaves coming to Canada.

It is telling that the North End's historical summits are the 1917 Halifax Explosion, a colossal man-made disaster, and George Dixon, a turn-of-the-century prizefighter of Homeric achievement, ruined by his era and his excesses.

Dixon was a photographer's apprentice from Africville. In his teens he moved to Boston, and by his mid-20s he had become the most famous black man in the world — the first black to win a world title and the first man of any race to win more than two world championships (bantamweight and featherweight). Dubbed 'Little Chocolate,' he was renowned for his skill and courage. He is also credited with developing shadow boxing and inventing the suspended punching bag.

Some estimate he fought more than 800 matches, a great number of them 'bareknuckle' and lasting 20 rounds or more. Many bouts took place while Dixon barnstormed from town to town, taking on local challengers in backrooms and beer halls where onlookers burned his skin with cigars, whacked his legs with clubs and routinely spewed racial slurs.

Dixon earned thousands of dollars for his title fights — compensation previously unknown outside the heavyweight division — and enjoyed the high life, spending money carelessly and using booze and opium. His marriage to a white woman, the sister of his manager, defied social mores and nearly ended his career, if not his life.

All this took an enormous toll. On a frigid January day in 1909, long after his titles were lost and his skills corrupted, Little Chocolate was found delirious in a New York City alley, wearing only his old boxing trunks, his fists bleeding from punching locked doors. He died of the effects of exposure a few days later, broke.

He was 38 years old.

Through the generations Dixon has been lauded as a major historical figure in Halifax. A community centre bears his name and his life story became, oddly enough, a musical.

During the First and Second World Wars the city and the North End thrived. Blessed with one of the world's best harbours, Halifax emerged as a principal Atlantic port for the Allies in both conflicts.

During the Second World War thousands of civilians joined the government payroll as port workers and supply personnel. A significant percentage of them were North Enders.

Journalist Robert MacNeil, who grew up in the city during that period, wrote in his autobiography *Wordstruck*, that Halifax society "was conditioned by the presence of generations of well-born, sometimes aristocratic, British officers and showed it. [Haligonians] looked to England for the real juice of our patriotism, our ideals of dress and manners, codes of honour, military dash and styles of drill, marmalade and gin, pipe tobacco and tweed. The shops were provincial, the hotels ungrand, the restaurants unsophisticated. Yet the town had much grace. From their lace curtains in the elegant gingerbread houses of the South End, from their comfortable mansions on the Northwest Arm, from their clubs and yachts and mess dinners, well-to-do Haligonians smiled with the assurance of prosperity."

Few North End families in the 1940s smiled with the assurance of prosperity. But as a place to grow up, the district offered a womb of community that held the world at bay for a while. Core streets, such as Creighton and Maynard, were racially mixed and significantly less tense than they would be in future decades when black consciousness rose to challenge the entrenched social order. White residents were generally better off than blacks, but scores of close, supportive relationships developed between neighbours of different colours.

"We all got along," says Bubby Adams, a black North Ender. "We had one thing in common — we were all poor kids. And we respected each other. I don't think I ever got into a fight from someone [using a racial slur] when I was in school. That started when I was in the Canadian Armed Forces [a decade or so later]. When I was a kid I never ever thought about that. We went to each other's homes, we were all friends."

"Respect!" declares Bill Godley, a white North Ender. "It isn't like it is today. In our neighbourhood [it] wouldn't matter what colour you were, how much money your father had, if your father was a politician. That meant nothing. It was what kind of a person you are and what kind of a person I am. What you did for a living had no bearing on it. If you needed a hand? Guaranteed. We didn't care [about race]. If you were with a bunch of guys and somebody said the word nigger, you'd be apt to go and punch them in the mouth for sayin' that. You just didn't use that — never. If you were in a fight with blacks —'you black bastard!' — yes. But never nigger. You didn't cross that line."

"[Gottingen Street] was different then," civic leader Buddy Daye reflected in the *Chronicle-Herald* in the mid-1990s. "The whole neighbourhood was like an extended family, and that's something I've always believed in. Anyone on that street could speak to you if you were misbehaving and you would listen to them."

"I grew up with a little girl next door," says Billy Downey, an older brother of David's. "They had a police dog, and I had a police dog. Wilfred Young [who became fire chief] used to hook the two dogs up in a little cart that he had for his granddaughter, and put the two of us in beside there — a little black boy and a little white girl. Those dogs used to pull us all over the city."

In the early 1940s George Downey and his wife Leotra lived in a stable but unspectacular three-storey, flat-roof structure on Creighton Street. From time to time it housed as many as nine kids of their own, plus nieces and nephews on extended stays. Then, with the couple both in their 50s, Leotra got pregnant again, for a final time. Their tenth child, David, was born in 1942, the seventh son of a seventh son, another mouth for George to feed. Named after a grandfather he'd never meet, he was blessed by a Catholic priest in the Downey's Baptist household. "My miracle baby," Leotra would beam.

George Alexander Downey was born in North Preston, Nova Scotia, in the early 1890s, into a large family raised by his mother. Unable to enlist in Canada's regular military because of his skin colour, George joined No. 2 Construction, Canada's only all-black battalion, and in the First World War served in France, England, Belgium and Germany. After the war he found a job with Halifax Gas Works. In his 30s he formed his own business and became a 'coal hawker,' delivering coal across the city on open, horse-drawn wagons. Frequently the older Downey children accompanied their father or his men as they pressed on in all weather, street-to-street, selling coal for 50 cents a bag. At seasonal peak he had up to four teams going.

"My father employed mostly blacks, but a few white fellas worked for him," says Billy. "There were shysters and sharp guys."

Business was good, so much so that other hawkers complained George was enticing their customers by filling his bags with more coal than city regulations allowed. But the authorities could never prove anything of the sort. It seems George, well-connected with friends who worked for the city, always knew when inspections were imminent.

Saturday nights George's crews would surrender their proceeds to Leotra who in turn would dole out their pay. "She had the brains in the family," smiles Billy. "My father didn't have too much education. [But] he was very smart." George's other business ventures included selling Christmas trees and vegetables.

In his latter years George Downey was highly respected in the immediate neighbourhood —Mister Downey — a familiar squire-like figure in a well-cut suit ready with an animated smile. It was different in his younger days. Indeed, Billy and David volunteer that their father was a philanderer. "We have a lot of half-brothers," says Billy. "[Halifax boxer and fight promoter] LeRoy Jones is my half-brother. We were supposed to have four half-brothers, and they say that there was a girl, too."

"My father had another daughter named Evelyn," adds David. "She's got the same name as my other sister — Evelyn. I have two sisters named *Evelyn*!"

Not surprisingly, any discussion of George's wayward conduct was forbidden in the Downey home. While there were whispers for years, most Downey children were adults before they learned the truth about their half-siblings. "When I went to my mom one time about that, I got a slap in the mouth," recalls David.

Then there was the hooch. One afternoon George had arrived drunk at the Community Theatre on Gottingen Street to watch old films of Joe Louis fighting Max Schmeling and Tony Galento. Several Downey children were in their seats in another area. When George ranted at the screen the cops were called. "So here come the police, Edgar Malay. He took him and put him in the wagon. We all rushed home cryin' and everything. 'They arrested Daddy! Mom! Mom! Mom! Mom! They arrested daddy!' She said, 'Dad's OK. He's just in the room sleeping.' [The police] used to do that all the time. So we all got to like Edgar Malay."

Despite such displays, George was a man of formality — a former serviceman who dressed impeccably on Sundays and insisted the dinner table be set to perfection. He was also the family disciplinarian. Five-foot-six, with broad shoulders and long arms, he possessed a powerful and decisive grip. "When we got out of hand, we didn't mind Mom, but we didn't want Daddy to jump on us," says Billy. "He used to have horse reins. He had a real firm hand. When he told you to do something, you either did it or you would get the strap. When he beat ya, he beat ya. On the back. The only thing he never ever did was punch us."

"Leather straps," adds David. "He'd double it, with a loop. And that comin' down on both sides, you are gettin' the *force* of it."

George met Leotra Tomlinson, about eight years his junior, around 1920 and married her a year or so later. Leotra's father was an Antiguan. Her mother was from Fall River, Nova Scotia, a predominantly black farm community about 30 miles from Halifax. Leotra was born in Nova Scotia, but spent most of her teen years with her family in Boston. She returned to Nova Scotia, where she graduated from Halifax Academy then taught school near Fall River.

Leotra Downey was a neighbourhood treasure, a gracious presence who coped with her husband's infidelity by embracing her religion. She was a long-time member of the Cornwallis Street Baptist Church, a fulcrum for countless black North Enders. Leotra was also a driving force in the local home and school association, and for many years an executive member of the ladies auxiliary in the Royal Canadian Legion. During the Second World War she often hosted and fed Canadian troops — black and white — in her home. For many soldiers and sailors Leotra Downey's hearty meals and convivial conversation would be the closest thing to their own home they would experience for months, perhaps years.

She did all this in addition to raising her own seven sons and three daughters, plus providing sanctuary to nieces, nephews and needy neighbourhood children.

The Downeys rarely locked their doors. As a result, some mornings Leotra and George would be startled to find sleeping bodies in their living room. Usually it was a friend of one of their children. "This place is a damn shelter!" George would complain. Leotra simply set another place for breakfast.

"She was a beautiful lady, a bright lady," recalls Bubby Adams, a childhood friend of David's. "She was very protective of her family. She was the type of lady, that if there were 10 people in her home, and she had one slice of bread, she'd share it with everybody. I ate a lot of meals in her home. She was one of the many ladies like that on Creighton Street."

While Leotra had no favourites among her children, her miracle baby occupied a special place. "I think that my mom was one of the greatest moms that lived," David says. "She taught me to go to Sunday school, she taught us to make sure our homework was done, and stuff like that. [She'd] do anything for us, especially for me."

When David was about four, one of the Downey daughters, Lillian, still in her 20s, died of leukemia. George and Leotra officially adopted her four-year-old son, Vernon, nicknamed Bunbun.

Despite the full house, the Downeys never compromised on their children's behaviour towards adults. Proper regard for elders was an inviolable rule. Contravention meant a conference with George and his horse reins. It was therefore no accident that older neighbours thought highly of the Downey children, who often sat quietly in the living room when visitors came over, engrossed by the lively discourse and the North End state of mind.

By the time of David's birth, the Downey family's financial circumstances were improving. George was more settled, working at the Halifax Armouries as a janitor, drawing a civil service paycheque. He even found government work for a son or two. Ever the entrepreneur, George bought one house, sold it, then bought another, also on Creighton Street. Indicative of their relative prosperity, after the war the Downeys had one of the first cars in the neighbourhood. They were also the first to buy a television set. Many afternoons the living room at 149 Creighton would fill with neighbourhood kids mesmerized by the shadowy black-and-white screen sometimes showing nothing more than the 'Indian chief' test pattern.

"I never had a brand new bike," reflects David. "It wasn't that I wasn't blessed, [but] we all had hand-me-downs. I had things handed down from my brothers. We had an emerald green suit that I think my brother George had that went down from him to Billy to Donnie to Bobby. For it to come down all those years, that's how good those fellas kept their clothes. Later I had new things. In the early years, everything was passed on."

Ever polite, young David ran neighbourhood errands. Like his brothers before him he delivered the *Chronicle-Herald.* Up at 7 am (when it was still dark in the colder months) ... down Cornwallis ... along Creighton ... half of Agricola ... on Gottingen ... up Gerrish ... to Charles. Two hundred copies, six days a week.

School was a different matter. He was adept at sports and well-liked, but by middle school he was distracted and undisciplined. He enjoyed math and his interest rose occasionally in science class — "I used to like birds, and that" — but he found classrooms intimidating and frustrating. By Grade 7 he would sit in class and daydream of sports, counting the minutes until the afternoon bell when he would dash to the South Park Street gym or the Halifax Commons where he and other kids would play tackle football with no gear. While school made him feel foolish, sports fed his young ego.

"I used to say I was going to be like [Olympic sprinter] Jesse Owens, running. I used to try and run and think that I was him. I loved all the rough sports. I *loved* it! Just the thought of seeing someone stride and catching the ball in the air, and then someone probably flippin' me over and me maybe landing on my feet, and knowing that I made that catch. I think that's the greatest thing in the world."

For young David and thousands of his contemporaries, the next greatest thing in the world lived in New York City. His name was Sugar Ray Robinson.

To be like Sugar Ray!

In the middle of the twentieth century no black athlete was more admired. Certainly no one so influenced successive generations of black males who saw the boxing ring as *the* channel to fame, wealth and dignity. Muhammad Ali called Robinson "the king, the master, my idol."

A glittering diamond of a man whom New York sportswriter Barney Nagler declared "boxed as though he were playing the violin," Robinson's career spanned three decades and 201 bouts. He was world welterweight champion once and middleweight champion five times. In his prime — and for a brief period after it —

Robinson was a symphony of grace, his footwork superior, his leverage and hand speed unmatchable. *Los Angles Times* columnist Jim Murray wrote, "If Nureyev was a fighter, he would do it this way."

The world beyond the ring was less harmonious. *New York Times* columnist Red Smith thought him enigmatic, "a brooding genius, a darkly dedicated soul who walks in lonely majesty, a prophet without honor, an artist whom nobody, but nobody, understands."

Nonetheless, his sense of style, image and place was extraordinary and indisputable. Robinson passionately embraced celebrity, fixating on his pencil moustache and marcelled hair. He was among the first high-profile fighters to command a socially acceptable entourage, improving upon the typically ragtag ensembles of previous champions. Indeed, his team set the standard. It featured a secretary, barber, masseur, voice coach, several trainers, dwarf mascot, manager George Gainford and beautiful women.

Oft-married, Robinson was almost as renowned for womanizing as for boxing. His showgirls! His flamingo-pink Cadillac! His Harlem nightclub! His fine suits!

To be like Sugar Ray!

Ultimately Robinson was a proud, intelligent man who knew his own worth and refused to be exploited. While he was nominally managed by Gainford and financed by a brewery magnate, Robinson alone governed his career. Promoters and other managers raged against his intransigence and his demands for high purses. Many came to despise his arrogance and, eventually, the man himself. Robinson knew it and didn't give a damn. "Promoters and managers will be glad to see the back of him," barked Boston trainer Fat Johnny Buckley. "He wanted every cent for himself and left nothing for nobody else. He squeezed you until the pips squeaked."

Robinson quit in 1955, but returned to the ring several times, usually to pay back taxes. He retired for good in 1965 at age 44, his skills greatly diminished, having spent his final years losing to opponents unworthy of him during his prime. Although he earned an estimated $4-million in the ring, by retirement Robinson was nearly destitute. He reinvented himself in show business, but the novelty wore thin. In his final years he was stricken with Alzheimer's disease. He died in 1989, unable to recognize family and friends.

Young Downey was dazzled by the promise of *la dolce vita* presented by figures such as Sugar Ray Robinson. His reality was something different, however. Discouraged and embarrassed by his academic failures — he would quit at age 16, in Grade 7 — he nurtured an identity as an athlete and a neighbourhood kid who you didn't mess with. In the 1950s North End schools had an ample supply of students deft with their fists. David engaged in several schoolyard battles, often with older kids. He says the encounters usually concerned nothing more than reputation, "but you *had* to have those scraps."

"David was one of the best — probably *the* best — on the street," says his pal Bubby Adams. "This includes guys who made reputations years ago who were a little leery of comin' up against him."

Rocky Jones as a youth travelled with a crowd that included David's cousin. "We were real hellions. We would get into any kind of trouble. [But] David didn't buy into that. David was always the one who didn't get into trouble. I think it was his style. I think it was the way be carried himself. He was not confrontational in any way whatsoever."

But when David did battle, his brothers seldom interfered, adhering to a family credo that each Downey had to make his or her own way. When he was about 12 a bully chased him home. Instead of sympathy from his brothers he was shoved from the house, back outside to fight. "I went back out and kicked the shit out of the guy and he never bothered me again."

Street fights were almost always *fist* fights. The North End code forbade kicking or pipes or knives or guns, although there were instances of all that. "In our neighbourhood there was always street fights," says Bill Godley. "On a Sunday, what would we do? We'd go to the bootleggers and play cards. But if you and some other guy got into an argument, you'd get up and go out to the backyard. One of you smacked the other fella a couple of times, and then you'd be finished and you went back in. There was no knives, no two or three guys jumpin' in. None of this kind of stuff at all. Also, if I beat you today, you didn't go get a cousin or a big brother to come after me. There was none of that. You were *you*."

North End street fights often entailed community honour and featured black-on-black at least as often as black-on-white. On occasion groups of youths from Preston, a black community 15 miles to the east, would turn up in the North End and the battle was joined. "Some of their names were the same as ours," shrugs David. "They were some relations to us, a distant cousin. They hated us because we were *in town*. It's because we were brought up different. Half of them guys out there didn't like me and I did nothin' to them. And the guys out the other way, from Africville, used to be the same way. Picking fights with my brothers and them."

One evening in a Gottingen Street poolroom a youth from North Preston was roughing up one of David's buddies. Soon the North Preston teen began to land hard, bare-knuckled blows to the face. Downey stood by quietly, alert to every twitch in the room. When the beating became too one-sided, he stepped forward.

"Hold it!"

A few North Preston boys inched closer. Downey turned to them, his arms out. "No one else is jumpin' in. He's had enough." The North Preston kid crunched a couple more shots into the face of Downey's friend. Blood now spilled from his nose and mouth.

"That's it!" shouted Downey.

The North Preston kid released his victim and took a couple of slow steps forward. "Enough's enough," said Downey. "You got him beat. There's no sense in you trying to kill someone, is there?" The last words were delivered with a sneer.

The North Preston kid knew of Downey's reputation, but he couldn't be seen to back down. Not in full view, anyway. "I got no beef with you."

Downey's response was icy. "If you wanna go, then shit, let's go. Take your shot ... but I'm not him."

The North Preston kid froze.

Downey moved to his fallen friend, helped him to his feet and together they walked out of the poolroom.

After he left school Downey continued to play sports, especially baseball. He was a member of the Vaughn Furriers when the team won the Nova Scotia and Maritime junior baseball titles in 1962. He played several positions, mainly second base and outfield. Touring the province with ball teams, Downey came across vitriol unfamiliar to him as a child on Creighton Street. For the first time he felt the emphatic division of race. A series against a team from Bridgewater, on Nova Scotia's south shore, was especially jarring.

"Our team, the majority of the guys were black, but not all of them. They were calling us niggers, and when we got down there the Mounties were all there. The [fans] said, 'No niggers are comin' here and playin' on that field.' Some of the other [black] guys on our team weren't taking this too calm. They said that if anybody bothered them they were hittin' them with a bat. The Mounties came in and they stopped it. It left a bad taste in my mouth."

While sports were a passion for Downey, girls were not. At least not in terms of a formal courtship. A late bloomer, his first serious relationship developed in his late teens when he became interested in a pretty 16-year-old from a respected family in Beechville, a black community on the city's western fringe. Downey moved cautiously, cowed by his innate shyness and by her mother, who watched from all angles at all times, wary that her daughter was sitting with this older North End boy with the sweet smile.

And aspirations to be — of all things — a prizefighter.

4

DEBUT

Summer evenings on the corner of Creighton and Gerrish streets spawned mock pugilism fuelled by equal parts testosterone and boredom. No neighbourhood adolescent ever discovered true virtue at this North End intersection, christened the 'Belt and the Buckle' by locals for reasons long forgotten. Yet in the late 1950s the location at least nurtured a simple, comforting camaraderie. Among the regulars were David Downey and his pal John Bruce, who lived above David in the middle flat of the Downeys' triplex on Creighton.

"Someone'd push John at me, and I pushed him back and he started sparring with me. And I'm sparring and throwing my hands out and we're slapping each other with our hands — bing! bing! — and the hands go out so quick and tap each other, not hit each other hard. And I'm catching his hand. And I'm moving. And I'm sayin', 'I'm Ray Robinson!' Bang-bang!"

Sometimes this looked all too real to the neighbours who'd call the cops who'd would arrive at the corner of the Belt and the Buckle to shake their heads and yet again order the boys to disperse. Which they would do ... until the cops were out of sight.

One night a middle-aged man came out of a nearby boxing gym and was fooled, too. "Jesus boys, enough now!" shouted Murray Langford. Downey and Bruce stopped their combat and explained. Langford recognized Downey, having noticed him at the gym watching his brothers. And around the neighbourhood he'd heard talk of this local kid with the nasty fists. Usually such talk was pure bullshit. Most street kids weren't worth the sweat. But this time he knew the family name and — with his own eyes — saw *something*.

"You guys ever think about boxin'?" Langford asked.

"You ask *him*," Downey replied, nodding towards Bruce. "I ain't got no interest."

Langford continued to press the teenager.

"C'mon Murray," said Downey. "Dad wouldn't let me do that. He's seen Billy doin' that, but he ain't gonna want *me* doin' it. [I] don't need to tell *you* about my dad."

Days later, with David in another room listening quietly on a bed, Langford stood in the Downey family kitchen and listened to George Downey's exasperation over his youngest son's aimless, unproductive life. "Let him go ahead," growled George, then in his 60s. "He needs somethin' to get him straightened out. He's no different than his brothers. Let him do it and get his brains splattered, too."

Leotra winced. "No! He's not doing it! George, he is not going in for boxing."

"It might straighten him out," George snorted. "He don't want to listen to people, so he can get his ass out of here. If he ain't gonna go to school … I'm tired of him tellin' me he ain't goin' there. If he don't do *something*, he won't be here in this house."

Leotra remained opposed to just the *thought* of large men disfiguring her miracle baby.

Langford persisted. "Look, Leotra, we won't let him get hurt. We just want him to do somethin'. Look, I bought him somethin'."

He showed her a pair of new boxing gloves, then some hand wraps, then a pair of trunks. She stared at the display. "Well, if he really wants to do it. But I wouldn't have thought that David would want someone beating his face in. He's good in sports, but I know him. He's quiet. He's different from the rest of my children. But I can't get him to do anything."

A few days later Downey joined Langford in the Creighton Street Gym, a minute's walk from the corner of the Belt and the Buckle.

The Creighton Street Gym nurtured the dreams of young men who otherwise had few. It was the brainchild of two New Glasgow-born brothers, lightweights Keith and Percy Paris — men of good intentions and limited capital. The enterprise reflected both qualities.

It was 24 feet by 24 feet, a precariously constructed, free-standing single-storey structure down a dark alley between houses. Halifax promoter Sonny MacPhee recalls, "It had a speed bag and a punchin' bag and a bad smell. Nothin' else." During relatively opulent periods it also contained a ring, a floor mat, a rowing machine and skipping ropes.

Tattered and discoloured boxing posters were nailed to the walls. Gloves were seldom in the best repair, but there were usually enough to mix and match. There was no running water, so fighters brought their own drinking water and took sponge baths in a corner, or used the shower in a house next door. All this for 50 cents a session or six dollars a week. Even then, some patrons stiffed the Paris brothers.

"We tried to heat with a pot-bellied stove," remembered Buddy Daye, a regular. "You could see your breath while training."

At one point the facility's official name became The Prizefighters Club, after the Paris brothers received a license for a club and lounge. It was also known as the 'Rock 'n Roll Gym' (motto: If We Can't Rock Ya, We'll Roll Ya).

Whatever its name and appearance, several proficient fighters trained there. Among them were Daye, Lennie Sparks and LeRoy 'Rocco' Jones. Most were black, but the clientele also included whites such as Blair Richardson and Canadian light heavyweight champion Yvon Durelle. Another white drop-in was Canadian lightweight champion Kid Howard, although his preferred club was a slightly larger facility near the harbour, aptly christened 'The Bucket of Blood.'

The Creighton Street Gym was a reservoir where on short notice Maritime promoters could pluck respectable opponents for main-event fighters. "There was a fella there one night," recalls MacPhee, "and they took him up to Bathurst, and I said to him, 'How did you make out?' And he said, 'Well, I won the fight. In three rounds.'

I said, 'How much money did you get?' He said, 'I didn't. I got a bottle of wine and I put it away and it froze and broke!' "

To save money, boxers of the Creighton Street Gym did their own booking, travelled together and acted as cornermen for each other. Over time this strengthened a sense of community already fostered by the veiled — and not so veiled — segregation of the 1950s and 1960s.

The apartheid required black fighters to secure special permission to work out with white fighters at facilities such as the gymnasium at Canadian Forces Base Stadacona. "[We] weren't allowed to hit them and we had to pull back on our punches," Buddy Daye told the *Chronicle-Herald*. "So back to Creighton Street we would go, where the real action was and the real wars were."

Roadwork was two or three laps around the Halifax Commons, then a climb up the steep grassy embankments of nearby Citadel Hill. In the gym, fighters ceaselessly evaluated one another, cutting loose on the heavy bag when eyes shifted their way. Spirited scraps were not unusual. "We trained pretty hard there," insists Percy Paris. "The guys would take advantage of you if you didn't."

And there was that *sound*.

"Sometimes in the gym you can hear the bing-bing-bang — you can hear that *snap*," says Downey. "I used to try and make that sound. And you can hear it — bang, bang-bang! When you hear that, you know you are hittin'. Can you imagine snapping somebody's head like that? You know you are scoring a punch. A rhythm."

Murray Langford heard Downey's rhythm. "Playin' a tune on the heavy bag," he often called it.

Music like Sugar Ray's.

Promise worth the sweat.

David Downey made his professional boxing debut on an eclectic but otherwise unremarkable card in May 1960. The main event featured square-jawed white hope Ted Doncaster, a New Brunswick light heavyweight. The undercard showcased a roguish celebration of life named Kenny Shea, a Dean-Martinesque band singer, shoe repairman, scratch golfer, fireman, snooker champion and, on at least one occasion, nude model.

Downey, then a welterweight, was in the preliminaries against Kenny Chinn, another welterweight, whom he had known casually for some time, and who lived a block or two up from the Downeys. Chinn was handled by local veteran Bob Talbot. "He was just a tough young white kid from Maynard Street," says Downey. "There was a section where there were mostly white families. He didn't care for none of us guys, and we didn't care for him."

In the Creighton Street Gym during the days leading up to their match, Downey began offering up conspicuous demonstrations of hand speed, *playin' a tune* for educated ears, especially Chinn's. But it was largely false bravado. At age 18 and with no amateur experience, Downey soothed his abundant self-doubt by constantly reminding himself that if he lost there was always baseball. He felt he was better at baseball, although his brothers disagreed.

The 'special four-rounder' lasted just 57 seconds into the second round. Reported the *Chronicle-Herald*, "Downey, a flashy boxer and puncher making his professional debut in the Forum ring, caught Chin (sic) off balance and dropped him for an eight-count in the first round. In the second Downey swarmed all over his rival with a flurry of punches and Chin went down for the full count."

A crowd of 3,500 watched. Downey's take was $80. "I took the money home to my mother and she was mad! She didn't know that I was gonna' be in that fight. I gave her half of the money.

The other half went in his own pocket and stayed there for some time. "I was like a king. [If I had only] four dollars to myself, that must have lasted me a couple of months. I had nothing, really. We always had stuff in house for food and things [so] I'd buy myself a bottle of pop or something. Once in a while an apple. But I just didn't have any need to spend it."

He won his second fight, about seven weeks later, against New Glasgow's Billy McIntyre, who fell in the second round under another series of punches.

"Impressive," noted the *Chronicle-Herald.*

Impressive? Suddenly Downey was seeing possibilities in all of this. Never had anyone written such a thing about him. He asked Langford to arrange another fight — soon.

Langford telephoned a Maritime stalwart named Peanuts.

Summerside, Prince Edward Island, native Walter 'Peanuts' Arsenault was five-foot-seven, 150 pounds, with what P.E.I. boxing writer Wilf McCluskey described as "the build of a sawed-off Hercules." By career's end he'd have 114 recorded fights — and maybe as many unrecorded — all without a manager. Once he fought three times in one week, and seven times in two months. Although he won more than he lost, Peanuts entertained no illusions of important titles. He just enjoyed a scrap.

He would battle in Boston and Quebec City and the like, but most of his matches were on Maritime soil where promoters knew he'd supply a good show and not squawk too much about fighting for — well — peanuts. Most efforts netted him only a couple hundred dollars, cash. His best payday would be $1,200 for taking on Clyde Gray, one of Canada's elite boxers of the 1970s. This was hardly income enough to support a family of five kids, so Peanuts cleaned the streets of Summerside and depended on boxing and its prank-filled travel to break the monotony — sleeping 13 in one room at a Black's Harbour, New Brunswick, motel or plotting with buddies to swipe boxing gloves from a Quebec City promoter.

Peanuts was no saint in the ring, either. "I *might* have used some dirty tricks a couple of times if somebody else used them, like a head butt or a shoulder or an elbow. But if the guy did it more than twice, I'd get pissed off and show him that I could do it, too."

Like many fighters of the era — when a medical history file conveniently travelled a good distance behind a hungry fighter — Peanuts could box at will, untroubled by regulations. Pre-fight medicals were casual, if they were carried out at all. "They'd usually check just your head."

Peanuts augmented his training with cigarettes, sex and wine. About the only thing he abstained from was protective headgear. "I used to train wherever I could find a place — in back yards, in front yards, an old cannery. I remember one time we were trainin' and there was a fence all around and there was this board with nails all through it. If you went against the fence, you'd get hit, plus you'd get a few nails in your back."

Downey beat Arsenault in a split decision. The match taught the 18-year-old a few tough lessons. In clinches Arsenault used elbows and drove Downey's chin upwards. "He was dirty, dirty! [He didn't] shave before the fight. He was in there rubbin' and rubbin' [his face against mine] and I'm thinking his face feels just like my dad's when he don't shave.

"After the fight I went after Murray Langford and them guys and said, 'What are you trying to do to me? He was trying to kill me!' "

Downey's first three fights had paraded his talents, but also exposed his vulnerability to more experienced fighters. To address this situation, in early 1961 his brothers pooled their money and subsidized a pilgrimage of sorts to boxing's Mecca — New York City. It would be Downey's first major trip and he became homesick.

"When I got there I met Murray's uncle. I was in the hotel and I didn't like staying there. I stayed in the Bronx on 149th Street and 3rd Avenue. That was a pretty good neighbourhood but it's rough all around there. If you're walking in the daytime, you're probably OK. But in the night-time ...

"I called home a lot because I didn't know no one. You're in New York. You are a teenager and you have to walk along the street. I was ready to pack up after I got down there after two weeks. [In] the gym they had Spanish people there, the Cubans, everyone's in their own little section. I couldn't speak Spanish, I couldn't speak Cuban. I can just speak English."

Downey's principal mentor in New York was Morris 'Whitey' Bimstein, known for his work with middleweight Rocky Graziano. The teenager was agog. "I'll never forget him there with the cigar. I'll *never* get over it. There was the same Whitey Bimstein!"

Bimstein was a stocky, obese, slightly stooped creature with bulging eyes and white lashes. He had become one of the sport's most coveted trainers and cutmen, albeit with methods that stretched the limits of even boxing's eccentric practices. To prevent cuts Bimstein would rub his fighter's face with petroleum jelly and carpenter's wax. To stop particularly bad cuts he used Monsel's styptic — a mixture containing iron subsulfate, thought to cause permanent blindness if it spilled into an eye. He stopped bleeding noses by stuffing adrenaline up his fighters' nostrils. During important fights he pierced swellings with a lancet and personally sucked out the blood.

By the early 1960s Bimstein was profiting nicely from this reputation. Moreover, in an opportunistic autumn-years change of attitude, he even began lauding the work ethic of the 'coloured boys.'

Downey still recalls the advice he received in New York. "They taught me how to hold my head. I was sort of copying [current heavyweight Floyd] Patterson with the peekaboo. I used to hold my hands up here [in front of my face]. Whitey Bimstein said what works for Floyd Patterson doesn't have to work for everybody else.

"He told me that Joe Louis could stand there and just grab a fly right out of the air, *boom*! So they used to [show] me that and I used to practice it. And they used to practice with me on the speed bag. After a while I was breaking more speed bags. When [I came] back here, people who used to train me would say to me that I was different."

Downey's workouts took place at Stillman's Gym in Lower Manhattan, four blocks from Madison Square Garden, in a neighbourhood where muggings were common, litter carpeted the streets and vagrants slept in front of liquor stores.

Stillman's reeked. Clients reached the gym up a gloomy, dark stairway. Reaching the top they were met with a stench that on its own seemed likely to inflict brain damage. Boxers smoked heavily and it was hard to see through the thick haze from one side of the gym to the other. Grimy windows, so caked with filth that they camouflaged into the wall, were never opened. According to legend, when heavyweight champion Gene Tunney one day requested that the windows be opened to get some fresh air, proprietor Lou Stillman refused, bellowing, "That stuff kills people!" Signs prohibiting spitting were posted everywhere, although Stillman violated the rule with practically every breath he took.

A former private detective, Stillman always packed a gun. "He was a strange man who would fart in public then go home and paint in oils," wrote promoter Teddy Brenner in *Only The Ring Was Square*. "Just why he wore a gun I do not know because there were no gangsters in the gym, not every day anyway. [He] ran the place from a high stool near two rings on the main floor of the gym. That was his office. A clock above him timed the rounds and there was a mike on a shelf by his shoulders. He had a voice you could hear above a crowd in Times Square on New Year's Eve. Stillman treated all fighters the same way — nasty. He always said, 'Treat them right and they'll eat you alive.' "

Stillman's clientele ran the gamut, from boxing sovereigns such as Joe Louis, Rocky Graziano and Joey Maxim to luckless wastrels from the slums. Crowds reaching 200 would relinquish a few cents to watch name fighters train. Sparring was savage. Newcomers were relentlessly tested.

"That gym was old and dirty," recalls Downey. "Everybody's showering at once. It was bad. The bathroom, the showers. The white enamel was all grey and green and slime. I had to take my shower, [but] I was gonna walk home [to do it]. And a guy there said, 'You can't go home, goin' on the bus stinkin' and smellin' like that. And people knowin' you're a fighter and lookin' like that. Ya gotta shower.' " So Downey showered wearing his sneakers.

Immediately after his tutelage in New York, confident and looking to earn a little cash on the way back home, Downey accepted a fight in Montreal against journeyman Claude Labonte. It proved an unfortunate decision. Downey lost. "He stopped me on a cut — my first cut. He butted me. I was doin' good. This guy was fighting six-rounders way before me, but I was beating him."

His makeshift corner — comprising his older brother Donnie and friend Lennie Sparks, both of whom happened to be in Montreal at the time — helped little. But poor corner or not, it was apparent Downey was still a work in progress.

Back in Halifax, a handful of men who were slowly becoming Downey's management team — for lack of a better term — arranged another bout, acting before the fighter could muster second thoughts about this whole boxing thing. Again Peanuts

Arsenault was summoned, and again beaten — by knockout, in the sixth.

Next up was childhood friend George 'Dookie' Munroe.

"Dookie was a flashy guy," laughs Bill Godley, a friend of Munroe's at that time. "Dookie would walk down the street singing his song — *give me a kiss to build a dream on, one caressing kiss before we part* — and he could sing! He was flashy and he loved the girls — white girls. Dookie was *so* smooth. I used to stand back and be amazed at him. He was a good guy, but he was smooth, he was shifty. He was hip for those days. Dookie stood out. If there were five guys walkin', Dookie would stand out."

A natural lightweight, a year or two older than Downey, the raffish Munroe had performed reasonably well against some competent fighters, including Buddy Daye in 1959. As his body filled out he had advanced from lightweight to welterweight and then to middleweight. By the time of the Downey fight, however, his prospects of advancing beyond club fighter status at any weight were remote. And that was not the only thing fading. When Downey first began training at the Creighton Street Gym, Munroe had appointed himself the kid's unofficial guardian. By 1961, thanks chiefly to the New York experience, the younger man neither required nor wanted Dookie's shield. A moment of clarity loomed.

"I liked him because he did things to help us guys out," Downey recalls. "But he was arrogant and he was moody and he would challenge anybody. Don't matter who it was. [Before we fought in the ring] we were out there fooling around like we always do in the street, sparring and I was getting the better of him. And he didn't like this. He didn't like what I was doing, making him look bad. We almost started to fight right there — in the street. They broke it up, all the guys around us."

Antagonism between Munroe and Downey infected others. In the gym, Munroe's trainer Bob Talbot almost came to blows with Murray Langford. Downey remembers even their fathers were confronting one another. "[Dookie's] father said that his son's gonna beat your son's head in. He was cocky. My father said, 'As long as your son has a hole in his ass, he'll never beat him!' They had to restrain [my] dad. We thought he was gonna have a heart attack!"

The fathers might have produced a better fight.

Downey hammered Munroe, winning with a third-round knockout. "I didn't even have a bruise on me. I was beating him and makin' a fool, and then I got him in the corner and beat him and knocked him down. I didn't *want* to hit him, I was embarrassed. I said, 'We're friends.' "

David and Dookie were never again close. "I wasn't that little boy he knew years ago."

The Munroe bout was Downey's only recorded fight of 1961. The next year he would also have just one fight — a second-round knockout in New Glasgow against a local fighter named Al McLean.

A career's pattern was settling in. Having laid the foundation of a promising prizefighting career, Downey suddenly stopped fighting. Except for a six-round exhibition against his friend Lennie Sparks in 1963, *The Ring Record Book and Boxing Encyclopedia* lists no matches for him during all of 1963, 1964 and 1965. He would not fight again until August 1966, when he would flatten nondescript Charlie LeGare in three rounds, then beat Peanuts Arsenault again.

The span of 50 months between bouts truncated an encouraging apprenticeship and disappointed those who had invested time, money and hope in him. Just stepping into a ring — even against plainly inferior opponents, even for negligible earnings — would have at least provided opportunities to learn. It also would have kept his name before the public, made him more marketable and broadened a following that, up to 1962, was mostly black. When he finally did return to the ring, many hardline boxing fans booed him. Although there would be future success, he never completely recovered from this peculiar, ill-timed, self-imposed exile.

Downey today is circumspect about the period. He claims to have had a few local, unrecorded matches but cannot recall when these fights actually took place. There seem to be no newspaper accounts. If the matches did occur, they were certainly not with 'name' opponents.

Regardless, Downey insists he was always *willing* to fight, but few offers came, despite the connections of manager Murray Langford and trainer Vince Hennebury, despite the favourable impressions he made while in New York and despite pressure from the local boxing authority and the public to keep the sport alive in the city. Proposals that did surface were for amounts he found insultingly low and — *à la* Sugar Ray — were promptly dismissed. "It was because of money," he says. "They didn't want to give me no money [and] they were trying to headline someone else."

The extended inactivity also invited unflattering comparisons with Blair Richardson, who even in retirement continued to earn praise and respect, casting a shadow on boxers across the region — especially Downey. Some journalists speculated that Downey feared Richardson and his thundering right cross. Others continued to salivate over the possibility of the two facing each other in a ring. "[A] Richardson–Downey fight would have been a natural," says Pat Connolly. "That could have been built into the most attractive fight that Halifax would have seen in 50 years."

The long interlude between fights also helped mould the media's perception of Downey as enigmatic and unreliable. It was through this lens that reporters would view his future actions. It ensured an uneasy relationship for the remainder of his career and beyond.

Meanwhile, a significant change had taken place in Downey's personal life. In 1962 he and his common-law wife Judy Gabriel produced their first child, David Jr. Suddenly, at age 20, he felt life's swift passage from boy to man. For some time he had worked at car washes and other odd jobs around Halifax for low wages and little satisfaction. Then one day, like countless thousands of Nova Scotians before him, he found government work by knowing the right somebody. The door opened when a politically connected family friend was driving along Gottingen Street and spotted the young man heading nowhere in particular.

Walter Sparks, a sharp dresser with sharp wheels, drove Downey to a government building downtown where Sparks introduced him to a smiling white man who eagerly clasped Downey's hand. "You're a helluva fighter," the man gushed.

Downey smiled broadly.

"We're gonna do somethin' for you."

Soon Downey was inspecting an application form. "I never filled one out before in my life. Walter helped me and he sat down, filled it out. Then we went back and he talked to the guy."

"Are you ready to start work?" the smiling stranger asked Downey.

"Yeah."

"They want you to report down here tomorrow."

Bemused by his good fortune, Downey returned the next day. That summer he helped maintain the yards around Province House, painted a brick wall and picked up garbage. The temporary work led to full-time employment where, as part of a small unit of men, he set up rooms for official functions. Sometimes he would relieve the building's parking booth attendant — often before fights so he would not hurt himself moving furniture. The parking booth assignment provided regular encounters with politicians who would bring him the odd snack of fried chicken and the like. Two cabinet ministers, Peter Nicholson and Garnet Brown, on separate occasions personally called Downey's supervisor and insisted he be sent home to rest for a fight.

Other times gestures were even grander. One day in 1975 a local businessman with political clout came upon Downey and casually asked whether he would rather see Muhammad Ali or Clyde Gray fight. Both had up-coming matches. Downey smiled and selected Gray's fight in Puerto Rico. The man then asked Downey to come and wait outside the premier's office. When he emerged he instructed the boxer to get ready to leave for San Juan and not to worry about the flight or the hotel. A few days later Downey was part of a small Canadian contingent watching Gray fight Angel Espada for the world welterweight championship in Roberto Clemente Coliseum.

Downey remained with the provincial supply and services department for 29 years, until his retirement in the late 1990s.

5

TEAM

By the time of the Meilleur fight, Downey had positioned his team around him. More convenient than strategic, it featured four men who inhabited different worlds within the compact boundaries of one city.

Manager Murray Langford and trainer Vince Hennebury were from the docks. Both would be with Downey for nearly his complete

Some members of David Downey's team (from left to right): Murray Langford, manager; Tom McCluskey, trainer; Downey; and Vince Hennebury, trainer (c. 1969).

Murray Langford and David Downey.

run. "They weren't movers and shakers, they were cornermen," reflects Pat Connolly. "They were people who really took their directions from David, instead of David taking his direction from them. So that allowed David to maintain total control of his own destiny. I don't think you can regard either one — with all due respect — as a manager, [someone] who knew the business well enough to push the doors open, to make bouts and make money."

His financial backer was Victor Beed, a successful local entrepreneur who on his own inclination shifted in and out of the cast, depending on whether or not his money was required. Promoter LeRoy 'Rocco' Jones was an urban scalawag and follower of the fight game who ostensibly operated independently. He was also Downey's half-brother.

By adopting such a passive quartet Downey likely shortchanged his career, in effect condemning himself mainly to prizefighting's second tier.

But fight people are hard to find. Especially good managers.

The good manager is a comprehensive impresario. He is his fighter's primary business agent. He negotiates contracts with an eye for top dollar and safe conditions. He lobbies governing bodies responsible for licensing and ranking. He forever seeks an edge for his man and leaves nothing to chance. He makes travel arrangements, inspects how tightly the ring ropes are drawn, examines the other fighter's bandages, watches what opposing cornermen apply between rounds, ensures tickets are set aside for his man's friends and family, deals with the media and ensures the dressing room is conducive to emotional preparation. And he makes certain his fighter gets to the arena on time.

The good manager is an iron-minded architect of his fighter's career. He selects opponents who will supply experience and pad his fighter's record. But, as Britain's best-known manager Mickey Duff avowed to American author Thomas Hauser in *The Black Lights*, "sooner or later you're faced with a moment of truth when your guy has to fight a real fight." The good manager does all this for 25 to 30 percent of the fighter's purse, according to boxing's customary practices.

"If you get a manager, you've got to get a manager with a heart," says Halifax promoter Sonny MacPhee. "You've got to get a manager that wants to take you somewhere. [You need] some guy that's doin' it for the kicks — got a few dollars to spend on ya — and would probably stick with ya. *If* you can find a guy like this."

David Downey never really seemed to look for a manager. Instead he *accepted* Murray Langford, for reasons simultaneously self-serving and self-defeating. "Murray was quite a character," MacPhee says. "I don't think [he] got a great deal of money out of it. Murray Langford did the best he could."

"I thought he was a really nice guy," says former boxer and local gym owner Percy Paris. "Once in a while he'd get mad and jump up on his heels. Some of the guys used to tell Murray what they wanted to do, and Murray was a little scared of them. He wasn't as strong as he was supposed to be."

Outside boxing, Langford was a dockyard pipefitter whose life path never veered from North End Halifax for any significant period or for any eventful reason. He lived for many years on the edge of the Halifax Commons, and was a member of both the local Prince Hall Lodge and the Cornwallis Street Baptist Church where he was a baritone in the choir. Raised by his mother, Langford was married and had a stepson. He fought with little distinction as an amateur or professional, but in the process learned the craft reasonably well.

And he had *the* name. Langford. As in Sam Langford, the Nova Scotia-born 'Boston Tar Baby,' the early twentieth-century great rated by *Ring Magazine* among the top 10 heavyweights of all time, and a cultural icon whose luminous career and tragic dotage forged both legend and cautionary tale. Murray savoured the bloodline that allowed him to claim Sam as a great-uncle and boxing as a genetic entitlement. The link bestowed a cachet otherwise unthinkable in such a routine life. Newspaper articles through the years never failed to mention his bond to Sam.

Before Downey, Murray Langford managed — in his own manner — a respectable cadre of prizefighters. These included Maritime heavyweight champion Cecil Gray and lightweight champion Percy Jarvis. He was also associated with Tiger Warrington, a popular light heavyweight from Liverpool, Nova Scotia, and Canadian lightweight champion Buddy Daye. Notwithstanding, his bond with Downey meant most to him.

Was he manager or trainer? Langford's role was never precise. Both he and Vince Hennebury worked both jobs, coexisting without rancour, accepting that neither would ever be exclusively in charge. Both understood that true authority on this team rested with the fighter himself. Like his imperious idol Sugar Ray Robinson, Downey viewed his career as a corporation with only one director on the board — himself. He innately understood the boxing adage: *the bell that tolls for all in boxing belongs to a cash register.*

Prizefighters had neither union nor any history of decent, fair representation. Downey was among a small percentage of boxers unabashedly determined not to join the long line of men, mainly from underprivileged backgrounds, despoiled by predators who lived off the blood and the brain tissue of their fighters.

"Boxers must remember that they are the employers and behave accordingly," Chris Eubank, a British middleweight champion, told a professional boxing association in the mid-1990s. "We engage managers to negotiate on our behalf and get the best available deal, but the contracts belong to us. We are the employers. We pay them [to] handle negotiations, so that we are freed from that worry and responsibility, but too often we are made to feel like the employee. If boxers don't ensure that every detail or every deal is reported back to them, they risk ending up bitter, twisted and resentful."

Downey was not about to take such a risk.

Between rounds, when trainers and cornermen usually do the talking, he essentially called the shots, changing strategy and directing his corner to watch for specific things. Of the two or three men in his corner, one was assigned to assess how things were going and to make suggestions. If Downey felt the advice unsound, "I pointedly told them I'm going to do something else. The ultimate decision has got to be mine."

Not only was Downey in command during fights, he often negotiated purses with promoters and largely steered the business end as well. As a child Downey had sensed money's power and witnessed from afar the respect accorded those who controlled it. He reasoned he was the central figure in his own boxing enterprise — the man risking *his* well-being in the ring — hence the revenue was *his* to control. He would reward and allocate it as he saw fit, boxing norms be damned.

Just as those on a high plane acquiesced to the practices of Sugar Ray Robinson, Halifax promoters and others soon understood Downey's process and often handed purses directly to him. He, in turn, apportioned Langford his share. He usually paid Langford and Hennebury $200–300 per fight — a flat rate rather than the customary percentage. He says both men were content with the arrangement.

"Dave's a funny guy," says Murray Sleep of Halifax, former president of the Canadian Professional Boxing Federation, and by chance Downey's immediate supervisor at his government job. "Dave would take anyone as long as he thought he could get away with paying them $20."

Downey recalls an incident involving the Forum commission and its accounting practice of stacking columns of $20 bills on a table — one column for each fighter on the card. Because he often helped count thousands of dollars at his brother's night club, Downey was constantly suspicious of the procedure. He frequently admonished Langford to always count the cash before putting it in his pocket.

"They had the money all there in piles. [W]e were supposed to get $1,500 or $2,000 that night for a fight — a 10-round fight. And they counted it out and it wasn't there. It wasn't there! I just stood there — and after me fighting and sweating and waiting and all that stuff, I said, 'If it's not there in the right amount of money that we signed for, I'm not touchin' nothin'. I'll sue.' They were short $300 or $400. [They] tried to shortchange me. They were trying to outsmart me."

Sleep, who was also a member of the Forum commission, agrees that no fighter was ever *overpaid*. "[Fighters and managers] would come in and demand their money right away. We used to try and get them to wait until the whole card was over. But some of them guys'd come in, like Rocco Jones and them, and demand their money. They wanted to go home."

Why stack the money?

"Maybe because they could do a little cheatin'," Sleep offers.

Whether Downey or Langford accepted the purses, money usually wound up with those who helped the fighter prepare for his matches. But according to Halifax trainer Tom McCluskey, getting paid by the Downey team was not a foregone conclusion. "I went along with him for a few fights. People that I did business with, people like Buddy Daye, Keith Paris, Dickie Howard and all that bunch, it was a different ball game. You'd help them, you'd do something for them, and the money was on the table. What they owed you the next day was on the table. With Downey it wasn't."

McCluskey says that in those days "five dollars or 10 dollars looked good to me," so he rarely signed a contract for any set amount for his services. He says this made things awkward with the Downey team as he chased his pay. "The next day I'd go see Murray and he says, 'See David.' I'd say, 'David never gave me nothin'.' You'd go see David. And [he'd] say, 'Murray is supposed to take care of you.' " As a result McCluskey says "many times" he was not paid. Downey ardently denies the claim.

As for Langford, if his managerial prowess rested somewhere other than with finances, it was definitely not in media relations — though Downey insists that both Langford and Hennebury took a stab at it, but sportswriters "would never show up." Langford was a reluctant interlocutor, perceived by reporters as a gruff, laconic man with a world-weary expression and little humour. He did not disdain reporters. He just showed no interest in them whatsoever. "He'd nod at me and growl," laughs broadcaster Alex J. Walling. "That's about it."

Langford seemed oblivious to how a comfortable association with reporters could advance a young athlete such as Downey. "When I met him, Murray was already a very old man — or at least appeared to be," says Doug Saunders, a CBC sportscaster at the time. "I could never fathom how much he did or didn't know about boxing. I'm certain that we never sat down for any long, meaningful discussions about anything. He didn't have a lot to say anytime I ever spoke to him. Not that he was ignorant, he was just very silent. He tended to play his cards very close to his chest."

Langford's effectiveness as a manager was further hampered by ill health — he was diabetic. Booze didn't help either. "We'd just ignore him," recalls Keith Paris, who saw Langford regularly at the Creighton Street Gym. "He'd come in and we'd wait until he went to sleep. He used to come to the gym and he'd have what he used to call a mickey. This guy would give him a drink and next thing — bang! — he'd fall off to sleep. We'd let him stay there 'til the mornin' and wake him up and he'd go to work at the dockyard. He was a good guy, training all the guys. We'd let it go because he was the type of guy you could depend on."

While a manager directs the career, it is the trainer who moulds the fighter. For 10 percent of the purse he conditions body and mind, develops techniques and strategies, and commands the corner during the fights. This intimacy between fighter and trainer requires more than routine compatibility. Good fighters and their trainers share a work ethic, a career objective and a bond rooted in trust and respect.

Sonny MacPhee describes that bond by citing Angelo Dundee, the celebrated trainer of Muhammad Ali. "Angelo Dundee could come in two minutes before [his fighter's] gonna go on and he'd come over and grab him by the shoulders and say, 'Now son, we're gonna make you champion of the world. You pay attention to every word I say. Never mind the rest of the shit. This is me and you goin' in up there. Come with me.' He'd put the towel on his guy's head and away they'd go. Between every round this kid would come back and [Angelo] says, 'You're doin' fine, but there's one thing.' He'd always give him that little confidence.

"I used to watch Janks Morton train Sugar Ray Leonard. Janks would be over in the corner and jeez, there'd be 2,000 people in there. Janks would say, 'Move to the left, move to the right, move to the left.' I said to him, 'Janks, Ray can't hear ya! I can't even hear ya!' Janks said, 'Oh, he can hear me.' I said, 'How the hell can he do that?' Janks said, 'Because he doesn't hear anybody else.' And Jesus, Ray'd hear every goddamned word. He was pickin' everything up. Boy-oh-boy! When you have a trainer and fighter on the same hook — fantastic!"

"Anyone can be a trainer," Tom McCluskey once told the *Chronicle-Herald*, "but to be a *good* trainer you have to love what you are doing. You have to be everything to a fighter. A trainer is a friend, a doctor and a teacher to a fighter. You can't work with a blueprint with a fighter — each one is different. [But] the boxer must have respect for the trainer."

In the 1980s, expose, *The Black Lights*, veteran American trainer Victor Valle explained that a trainer must demand respect.

Otherwise there will be no interest in what the trainer is teaching. "Sometimes fighters get like a mule and don't listen to nobody. That's when you tell them, 'If you don't listen to me, you don't need me. Goodbye.' [A trainer must also] show the fighter that he cares. That's not a machine out there. You don't stick a tape in a fighter and send him out there to fight like some kind of computer toy. You got to show your fighter some love."

Trainer Vince Hennebury cared. No one doubted that. Do you need a hand? Find Vince. Are you short a couple of bucks? Go see Vince. It's just that Vince Hennebury was a far better man than he was a trainer.

Cape Breton-born and about five-foot-ten, his sturdy facial features by mid-life were eroded by decades at the dockyards and by liquor. "When he'd come over and he was drinkin', we used to forget about him," says Keith Paris. "When he trained them, he trained them. When he drank, he drank. You just kept away from him, and they kept away from him."

Boxing was Hennebury's passion. He boxed a bit in his youth, and continued all his life to enjoy the sport, exhibiting palpable comfort around it. City gyms allowed him sanctuary. No matter how crude the practitioners nor how bleak the ambience, Vince was always there.

"[He] was dedicated to what he did," Sonny MacPhee affirms. "For starting out he was all right. Usually a fighter will go through two, three, four trainers, because somebody takes you this far, somebody takes you this far, and it's like a stepladder. A kid could come into the gym and Vince would say 'get into the ring and put some gloves on.' Great, great fella. Vince was what a neighbourhood needs."

Hennebury entered David Downey's orbit gradually. Newspaper accounts began mentioning him a year or two after the Kenny Chinn fight, when Hennebury was in his 60s. They labelled him the trainer, but those who witnessed the Downey-Hennebury association easily concluded that Downey mostly trained himself. Certainly Hennebury helped, but Downey devised his own fitness regime and sometimes even arranged for his own sparring partners.

"Vince Hennebury used to come down to my house and lay me down and put cotton batten all around the inside of my eyes and bathe it all over with fish brine, around my eyes so I wouldn't cut. The salt would draw your skin tight. This man knew what he was doin'. Yet, when the showdown came, *I* was tellin' *them,*" says Downey.

"Lovely gentleman," says Tom McCluskey of Hennebury. "A very fine man. Very limited on boxing. A good guy to have around. A good guy to go get the water bucket."

Pat Connolly first met Hennebury in the 1940s and came to know him well when he was doing boxing broadcasts in the 1960s. "I was doing a lot of the radio boxing stuff, and Vince was always around — on undercards. Vince was always the guy who came up with the four-round fighters. He'd show up with some new kid for a four-rounder or a six-rounder. I always thought he was more of a good guy who loved the game and was looking to spend a lot of time with the athletes, spend a lot of time with the kids, looking for his own star at some point."

Downey acknowledges that both Hennebury and Langford were heavy drinkers. "I [couldn't] stop them. When they were doing things through the gym, and when I was getting ready for fights, they wouldn't be drinking. But sometimes, right up to my fight night [they] used to have to have that drink in 'em." Downey would try to reason with both men, pointing out they were of little value during a fight if they were drunk. And he would worry, *"If I get cut, then what?"*

A third element in a fighter's team is the money man. He perceives the fighter as a commodity, an investment to appreciate in value. And he demands a clear plan that other members of the supporting cast must execute. Victor Beed was David Downey's main money man.

In the 1960s money men came in myriad forms. Many were mob-connected, drawn to the sport that readily accommodated a morality similar to their own. In Halifax, however, investors with or without underworld ties did not exactly row into the harbour on the hour. Especially ones willing to toss a bundle at a black kid with a Grade 7 education and no amateur pedigree.

While Downey's early matches displayed indisputable skill, it was obvious that progress required more instruction in the rudiments of the sport. His brothers tried to help by pooling their resources and sending him to New York and to Whitey Bimstein. But such efforts were a pale substitute for calculated long-term investment — a notion Victor Beed understood perfectly.

Beed was born in Halifax. During the Second World War he served overseas in the army medical corps and was injured in the bombing of England. He later returned to serve across Europe.

Beed's money and social standing flowed from diligence, shrewdness, generosity and a string of splendidly successful businesses he owned in Halifax and around the province.

The Olympic Gardens — which he co-founded with his father, John, upon returning to the city after the war — was a large, prosperous dance hall and amusement facility a few blocks from the Halifax Forum. Shelburne Shipyards, Elderbank Mines and the upper-crust Halifax Jubilee Boat Club were other Beed concerns that did well. He also owned the Carleton Hotel, where he opened the Jury Room Lounge, and the Seahorse Tavern. As a result of these enterprises, Beed was one of the province's largest employers of musicians. He also tried his hand in sports promotion with Halifax Raceway Limited and by sponsoring ball teams — and boxers.

Downey had observed Beed and his close friend, Dartmouth entrepreneur Fred Lahey, when as a youngster he squeezed into the Forum for the contests of Kid Howard and others. "We used to see the two of them. They were big shots. They were down at ringside for all the fights. I used to see them with their wives. She'd have a fur and he'd be in a suit and they'd bring them right down to the front row. We'd say, 'Look, there's all the money people down there.'"

Beed did not know Downey personally in the early years, but had seen him box a time or two. Finally, one day Beed invited him to his office, simultaneously impressing and befriending the young man by offering him *carte blanche* at his restaurant.

Undoubtedly Beed knew a tax write-off when he saw one. He assuredly understood that Downey — or any boxer for that matter —was unlikely to break even as an investment, let alone generate significant profit. But Beed was apparently content to pay for the fighter's training excursions — he handled expenses for Downey's trip to Boston to prepare for Meilleur — and to buy new equipment. And to generally enjoy the ride. So for the next several years Beed was the closest thing Downey would have to a legitimate backer, albeit one who preferred to remain behind the scenes.

Around the time of the Meilleur fight the press began referring to another man, Dick Fry, as Downey's "owner." By any measure, Fry was a peculiar choice to front as a prizefighter's owner. Gentle, white and in his 60s, he launched his music career by playing piano accompaniment for silent movies in city theatres. The prominent organist also became a local television personality during that medium's infancy in Halifax. He was a fixture in Beed's Carleton Hotel, where his piano contributed atmosphere. In an epoch of race riots, LSD and Jefferson Airplane, he favoured songs from *No, No Nanette. Tea For Two* was his signature piece. On radio his staple was nursery rhyme tunes.

The selection of Fry, yet another man who struggled with alcohol, did not please Downey. "I couldn't make sense of him." Fry always checked with Beed whenever Langford or Hennebury wanted something for their fighter. "I said, 'Murray, I can't do this. He doesn't know what we want, or what we're doin'. And people call him from the States for fights and things, and he has to go to Victor anyway."

While Downey's association with Beed lasted most of his career, to the relief of the fighter the Fry era was brief. Other than a couple of inside-page references in *Chronicle-Herald* articles, the organist soon faded into the background.

The fourth person in Downey's support team was Rocco Jones. While never a formal member, Jones promoted most of the major fights in Downey's career. For a long time it seemed that in the entire city of Halifax the two had only each other.

Before he tried his hand at promoting, the neon spectacle they called Rocco was himself a prizefighter. A mirthful kaleidoscope of twitches, shimmies and flashing combinations, Jones rarely reached the main event, not even in the 1950s when the sport in Halifax was at its zenith and there were wonderful crowds and pro cards twice weekly at the Forum.

So partway into a career too few people acknowledged, Rocco turned up the sizzle and began entering the ring in high white boots, silver trunks, red tassels and gaudy robes. The moves ... the bum wiggle ... the prancing ... the primping ... the head feints!

"Rocco! Rocco! Rocco!"

Born in 1933, reaching only Grade 8, Jones and one sister were raised in the North End by their mother. His father was George Downey, who through the years had little to do with LeRoy. The matter simply was not discussed in the Downey home. Once when a promoter proposed a fight between Billy Downey and Rocco, George Downey objected so ardently that the fight never happened.

The sweet-faced urchin was introduced to boxing when a local fighter named Kid Parsons one day escorted him and some used gloves to his backyard. "I just got goin' and I thought, 'I can do this!' " His *beau ideal* was neither Joe Louis nor Ray Robinson, but Kid Gavilan, a 1940s Cuban lightweight celebrated for his wild ensemble, anarchic attack and cheerful vulgarity.

In his prime Jones was a rung above club-fighter rank. Briefly managed by Vince Hennebury, he made his base the claustrophobic Creighton Street Gym, where he sweated elbow-to-elbow with choice pugilists such as Canadian lightweight champion Kid Howard.

Jones fought as an amateur, "but it wasn't much, about 40 fights. They didn't keep records." He had close to 100 pro fights, mostly four- and six-rounders. He knows only that he won more than he lost. "They didn't keep good records then, either." Nonetheless he cultivated a local following of citizens whom he regaled with the extravagant and the preposterous. The Halifax Forum's program, *Sports Weekly*, referred to him as "a crowd pleasing battler" and "the dusky Halifax scrapper."

Chronicle-Herald columnist Ace Foley observed "his whirlwind and unorthodox style."

"There was a touch of WWF in LeRoy," smiles Pat Connolly. "He got in and paid the price and entertained the folks and took some brutal beatings. He always ended up on his feet and would come back the next month for more. So there were some admirable qualities about LeRoy. And he loved to fight. Not a great fighter, but a good fighter."

"I took him up to fight [Canadian featherweight] Davey Hilton in Quebec," recalls trainer Tom McCluskey. "He was a character, an outright character. Good as gold, never even knew how to be bad, no thievery in him. No bad hate in him. Big white boots up to here. Always in good shape, throw punches all over the ring. Throw junk here, throw junk there."

"You never knew where he was comin' from," smiles Murray Sleep. "He'd come from the floor and hit you. He was comical."

"To me," says Percy Paris, "he was more like a comic than a fighter. Too flashy."

"I went out there to fight," states Rocco. "The flashiness came after a while."

What did not come were purses, at least enough to make it all worthwhile. So in the early 1960s Jones retired and opened a string of fight schools and gyms bearing names such as The Diamond Club and The Leroy Rocco Jones School of Boxing. One of his gyms operated on weekends and evenings in the 'B' block at Mulgrave Park. Some participants were as young as three, most were aged 14 to 17. No boy was refused entry, whether or not he had the 25 cents admission fee. Like all his enterprises it eventually folded — "We lost money in the five fights we staged. There wasn't any crowd support," Jones told the *Mail-Star.* But Jones was convinced it helped reduce vandalism in the neighbourhood.

In the mid-1960s he dove into what had become a local boxing vacuum and declared himself a promoter. The game — *his* game — required a little splash, he reasoned. And who around knew more about splash?

Jones became the most active fight promoter in the city during the period, forming a *de facto* coupling with its most prominent fighter — David Downey. Downey headlined Jones' first and last promotions and several in between. Between the mid-1960s and the mid-1970s he promoted about 10 cards, most of them in Halifax.

"Guys weren't fighting," explains Rocco. "Same as boxing is now. David wasn't doing anything. He had a title and he couldn't do nothin' with it."

He obtained his license from the Halifax boxing commission. According to Jones this made him the first black boxing promoter in Nova Scotia. "We did all right, but it got tougher as it went along. [The commissioners] pushed their authority. Things didn't suit them. They brought in different rules, like there had to be so many fighters on the card. [But] I got along all right because I was puttin' on good shows."

The Jones promotional machine was a modest venture comprising only LeRoy and his wife, Margaret, who typed contracts and the like. LeRoy did the rest, including some brassy negotiating. He usually offered fighters $100 a round. "For a six-rounder some of the guys would hold out. If you needed them, they'd get you up to $800. Downey, we put him on a percentage. He'd ask for a lot of money. He'd hold out. He had the crown and he wanted to get paid more."

Jones claims that finding money for promotions was not a problem because he kept his overhead low. But dealing with the local boxing authority was no joy. "The commission said you had to have money to cover this and to cover that. The guarantees! You had to guarantee a four-round fighter $50. You have to have this, you have to have that, you have to have everything. I think I did what was necessary. I don't think I did too many mistakes. I couldn't get the press to promote the fights. A successful promoter? No. I didn't get started off right."

"As I recall, LeRoy's biggest problem was that he was always under-financed," says Pat Connolly. "But LeRoy kept it going — at great expense to the (Forum) management. He filled a void. He kept it going when boxing was at a low ebb. Every time I turned around LeRoy was on my step with his handwritten press releases."

"He was a real character, but a very, very likeable person," says Tom McCluskey. "He couldn't promote nothin'. My God, it was a sin. He used to get drunk and get all goofed up and he got on the bottle there heavy. He'd phone me to get this fighter and get that fighter and before you know it the fight would be called off. He was crazy, but I liked him. He was a good guy."

His desire to see cards proceed despite obstacles — regulatory and otherwise — sometimes called for spontaneous ingenuity. Once at a weigh-in Jones suddenly realized he did not have a set of scales. So along with some buddies he rapidly produced a make-shift partition and laid a sheet of cardboard behind it. Jones then had the fighters walk around in back of the partition and step on the cardboard. "One forty-seven and a half!" Rocco shouted with a straight face. The fighters quickly stepped back out in front of the partition, smiling sheepishly. The reporters on hand were none the wiser.

"He was one of those typical dressed-up roosters," says May Bricker, the wife of trainer Frank Bricker, of Brantford, Ontario. "Always tryin' to make a buck or get into somethin'. He was honest — I'll say that. He never tried to give us any trouble like some of them did in the States. We really only knew him to go to the fights and come out again. He was sort of out of his depth."

To put it mildly.

People often weren't paid, states Sonny MacPhee, who promoted Halifax cards after Jones stepped away from the business. "He'd go out and get anything and talk the kids into signin'. 'I'm a little short on money. Sign for a dollar. I'll pay ya 500. Sign for a dollar.' Jeez, they didn't even get the dollar!"

MacPhee recalls that during a Jones promotion in Moncton, New Brunswick, in the late 1960s things were so badly bungled that the chairman of the local commission faked a heart attack and went to the hospital in an ambulance just to get out of the building. "Rocco was a fella that *wanted* to be a promoter, but never got to *be* a promoter."

Broadcaster Doug Saunders agrees. "He wanted to do the right thing and didn't have a clue in hell about how to go about it. It's too bad that he didn't have a partner who was strictly a businessman. He was very well-intentioned but inevitably — perhaps because of his style — things blew up in his face."

6

BENEVOLENCE

The lessons at Stillman's and at other New York gyms aided Downey's victory over Jimmy Meilleur, deep in the Black Power summer of 1967. But unfortunately for the Halifax fighter, the triumph coincided with significant problems for the sport.

Boxing was becoming isolated within North American popular culture. This growing estrangement sprang from many sources.

In the 1950s televised fights ate into live attendance, and in the 1960s closed-circuit television further distanced fans from fighters. Public fatigue with corruption and scandal in the sport were also taking their toll. Moreover, in the dawn of political correctness, many saw the sport as barbaric — a view fed by mounting and credible scientific evidence that boxing was simply too dangerous and should be banned.

The global decline in interest went into free fall in 1967 when boxing's charismatic prince, Muhammad Ali (né Cassius Clay), was stripped of his heavyweight title for refusing to be inducted into the United States military and stopped fighting.

In Canada, boxing was now unmistakably a secondary sport, burdened by a moribund national organization and lacking a major figure around whom it could rejuvenate.

Halifax remained a focal point of Canadian boxing. Sustained by historical and cultural links, the city continued to produce a disproportionate number of Canada's better fighters. It also led the country in safety standards — a noteworthy achievement given that this was certainly not the case just one generation before. But even in Halifax facilities were deteriorating and fewer youngsters were participating.

The decline across the region was instantly discernible. In 1960, when Blair Richardson won the Canadian middleweight title, he immediately became a figure on the national sports landscape. Seven years later, the championship claimed by Downey was diminished by indifference and tarnished by the sport's tiresome shenanigans, which marginalized both boxing and boxers.

Yet for those who truly believe, there is always hope, and every interesting new face brings proclamations of a resurrection. Ace Foley gushed that Downey's "natural speed and enthusiasm" could eventually make him "a magnet at the local gate. It could be the start of a boxing revival."

Just 36 days after he won the championship, the 'revival' continued when Downey was awarded a split decision in a match at the Forum over Manny Burgo, a former New England welterweight champion. The fight was tough and the decision was given a mixed reception. Only 1,500 came to watch Foley's 'fan magnet.'

Hope for a Downey-led resurgence was short-lived. He did not fight again until July 1969, when he made his first defence of his championship — 22 months after winning it. The usual reasons were given for the hiatus.

The defence was against long-time friend, Stewart (Stu) Gray.

Gray was the fifth-oldest of 13 children, born and raised in Three Mile Plains, a ragged township near Windsor, 40 miles northwest of Halifax, where he was educated in Nova Scotia's last segregated school. Growing up, Stu saw himself as a boxer, although few others in the community felt the polite, heavily muscled youngster possessed the raw aggression of a prizefighter. Certainly his mother didn't see it. Cora Gray agonized when any of her sons stepped into a ring, even the more talented ones like Clyde, a promising welterweight. She generally stayed away from Stu's matches.

"Stu would give you anything, he'd treat you A1," says Keith Paris, a long-time chum. "If you'd do something for him, he'd buy you a suit or a pair of shoes."

David Downey, sunglasses in the background, along with (from left): Murray Langford, Vince Hennebury, Tom and Cora Gray (parents of Stu and Clyde Gray) and Jay Davis.

"We used to go to the dances in Windsor and things like that," reminisces Downey. "He was a nice-looking guy. He had a way with the women. I used to laugh at him. He used to say, 'C'mon David, let's go over and see who could get this one or that one.' "

Friend or not, Gray was eager to challenge. And in a rare display of backbone, the Canadian Professional Boxing Federation pressured Downey to defend his title.

"I didn't look for this," says Downey. "But he was starting to put weight on and I figured he would have went for the light heavyweights rather than do this. I *knew* he couldn't beat me — I *knew* this. [I didn't] want this to happen."

Troubled by the thought of trading punches with his friend, Downey visited Cora Gray before he signed for the match. "Stewart wants this," he explained to her. "They're not giving me much of a choice."

"I know," she said.

"I hope you're not gonna be mad at me."

Cora smiled. "If you win the fight, I won't be mad. I'm prayin' for both of you."

Why Stewart Gray merited a title shot is unclear. His main qualifications seemed availability and a willingness to accept the terms of promoter Rocco Jones, the former Halifax lightweight staging his first card. It certainly was not based on his record, an uninspired five wins, eight losses, and two draws. But at least Gray was active. In 1968 alone he had seven fights, though most were against men of extremely modest credentials.

Ultimately Gray was a crowd-pleaser — a competitor who could withstand a severe pounding. In the tongue of the craft, he had 'heart.' Against Downey this was a dubious virtue. The contest between good friends was one-sided and, in spots, cruel. Downey was quick and sharp despite his layoff, dominating with superior skills that allowed him to move in, deliver brisk bursts of punches, then back out before Gray could respond. The fight was stopped in the eighth. Gray's face looked as if it had been through a blender. Downey's was unmarked.

"Gray came back with a fine display of courage," reported Ace Foley, "and never stopped trying."

"He went back home to Windsor and laid in bed for a week," recalls Downey.

"Stu was outclassed," insists Tom McCluskey, who worked in Downey's corner. "With Downey's speed we could go out there and stay a notch ahead — what we call a *notch*. This is what you do in the boxing game because of speed. You go out and set the pace because of speed. Stu was hardly in the ball game at all."

Months later Gray told the *Edmonton Journal* that he took the Downey fight on short notice and had to drop 16 pounds in three weeks. "I was too weak and lost the fight."

Tragically, Stu Gray would soon lose another fight, this time for his life. He collapsed following a Canadian light heavyweight title match with champion Al Sparks on a cold February night in 1972 in Winnipeg. It was the biggest payday of his boxing career — $2000 — but Gray was grossly over-matched. Less than a day later, he was dead.

From left: David Downey, Billy Downey and Canadian welterweight champion Clyde Gray.

Gray–Sparks was the main event on an appalling card, sloppily assembled by novice promoter Jack Keller, a Regina cheese salesman. Equipment for the matches was scavenged at the last minute. At least two of the three preliminary fights were fixed. At one point during the card, proceedings were delayed for an hour while Keller and Gray's manager Irving Ungerman squabbled in the arena box office over money.

The death was the subject of an inquiry by Manitoba county court judge Benjamin Hewak. In his report Hewak condemned the local boxing commission and criticized Ungerman, a Toronto chicken magnate who also managed heavyweight George Chuvalo, for his lack of co-operation with the commission and the police. He concluded that Ungerman's testimony had been "often evasive, at times inconsistent and on occasion simply untrue."

Gray's body was flown home to Three Mile Plains.

The prospect of doing battle with Stu's younger brother Clyde hovered over Downey in the early 1970s. The Canadian welterweight champion, Clyde Gray was the most successful Maritime fighter of his generation. While still a teenager Gray had left Three Mile Plains for Toronto, where he fell under the management of Ungerman. Despite personal conversations between the two fighters, Clyde Gray and Downey would never meet in a ring. Gray's busy schedule and irresolvable money issues were the two prime reasons why.

Cora Gray was relieved.

Boxing in Canada in the 1960s and 1970s was haphazardly governed and porously regulated by loosely connected commissions, bodies and authorities of varying repute and expertise. Such jumbled governance harmed the sport in a number of ways. Regulations to safeguard the health of boxers were applied partially and arbitrarily. "A bunch of junk," according to Halifax's Murray Sleep. Managers and trainers were self-appointed. Many promoters were inept or unscrupulous. Referees, cornermen and judges were frequently incompetent and poorly trained. Purses were meagre for anyone other than a select few fighters.

Remedy was difficult. Especially so because the public seemed to hardly care and the media typically looked away, convulsing briefly and furiously only when a boxer was seriously injured.

Such a fury arose following the death of lightweight Cleveland Denny in Montreal in 1980. Denny, formerly of Guyana, was beaten pitilessly over 10 rounds by Quebecer Gaetan Hart on the Duran–Leonard undercard. The tragedy triggered a federal government task force on boxing that, according to chairman Dr. Clarence Gosse, a former Nova Scotia lieutenant-governor, sought "to streamline everything so there is some semblance of uniformity in boxing, and try to make the sport safer as well as more appealing for those watching it."

The task force traversed the country in September 1980, listening to impassioned testimony and reflections on the sport. Halifax was the first stop, with a six-hour assembly at the Nova Scotian Hotel off Barrington Street. Not surprisingly, much of the testimony flowed from veteran fight men uneasy with drastic measures aimed at their beloved pastime.

"I would caution you not to overreact to the situation," Bruce Stephen, then chairman of the Nova Scotia Boxing Authority, urged the commissioners.

"I have been at this since I was 12 years old," trumpeted Halifax trainer Tom McCluskey. "I have yet to see a death [or] a serious injury, and I think in the Maritime provinces the boxing commissions are the best that I have come in contract with, and I have travelled quite a distance. We have had beautiful boxing matches in Halifax — professional. Everybody got their money's worth and they went home thrilled to death."

Defensiveness was not limited to the witnesses. Task force commissioner Clyde Gray, whose brother Stu had died eight years earlier following a match, queried, "Fighters have died before and there have never been any changes made. I just wondered why, all of a sudden, all these changes now that Denny's dead?"

Nevertheless, in often-bizarre testimony the process did illuminate several problems — most related to conditions in the sport in the 1960s and 1970s.

Referees were described as ignorant and physically unfit. Clyde Gray volunteered he'd seen referees in the ring "stinking of booze." The task force also heard that a couple of Nova Scotian referees had just one eye — information that stunned Rudy Ortego, president of the World Boxing Council's referee committee, present for the session.

Judges came under fire, too. "I have seen judges sitting there and having a great conversation while the fight was going on," testified George Borden, a long-time Nova Scotian referee. "I have seen guys forget what was going on altogether because some of them at their age don't remember too well."

Many cornermen were deemed incompetent. More than one witness recounted smelling booze on their breath as they attended to their fighters during a match.

Mostly though the task force struggled to understand Canadian boxing's hopelessly tangled web of authorities. "We are dealing with [three things here]: the provincial authority, the local commissions and the Canadian [Professional] Boxing Federation," said Bruce Stephen. He explained that the CPBF had jurisdiction only in Canadian title fights. This left local commissions as the authority for all the other matches. As a result, a fighter could work in Halifax under the rules of the Halifax commission and then go to Montreal, which possessed different rules and medical regulations. "[So] you are not clear on what we are dealing with."

"If the city commissions don't co-operate," warned one national official, "we're just whistling in the dark."

Veteran manager Red Forhan testified that "all local boxing commissions should be abolished as soon as possible. [They] lead to confusion, disorder, duplication and a breakdown in communication. Appointments to boxing commissions should not be based solely on political tie-ups or connections."

Even within Nova Scotia the situation was inconsistent, with separate commissions in Halifax, Dartmouth, Cape Breton and Pictou. In locations that had no commissions — such as Liverpool, Bridgewater, New Germany and Sheet Harbour — renegade cards were common.

"For each city and town," said Murray Sleep, CPBF president from 1979 to 1982, "if I went up and said, 'Look, you should regulate this boxing, there's nobody to regulate it,' they'd get a few fellas who would know a little about it [and] they would form these small commissions."

The muddle was similar in other provinces.

Atop this shaky pyramid was the Canadian Professional Boxing Federation. "The so-called Canadian Professional Boxing Federation is an empty concept that should either be endowed with power or scrapped by the federal government," United Press Canada sports editor David Tucker wrote at the time of the hearings. Few disagreed. It was obvious that the CPBF had little impact on the sport in Canada and virtually no control or power over local boxing associations or commissions.

While projecting the pretence of a higher command, in fact the CPBF was merely one component in a labyrinth of groups that operated more or less independently. Its main activity was to sanction national championship fights. "When they'd put on championship fights, the CPBF used to send a supervisor down and he'd take over from the local people," says Murray Sleep.

Another result of the sport's rudderless stewardship was that idle champions were seldom stripped of their crown. In the case of Downey, it was *twenty-two months* from title to first defence: how could a fighter retain a national championship given such idleness?

Many champions were indifferent to CPBF admonishments to defend their titles. Downey was warned several times, but so were others, including light heavyweight champion Leslie Borden of Montreal, and heavyweight champion George Chuvalo (although Chuvalo appeared to have an exemption because the CPBF felt he was too far above his competition).

The CPBF had a membership of roughly 200 and published ratings periodically — monthly at one point — but these were rarely carried by the media and therefore seldom seen by the public. Head office was "wherever the president was," according to Sleep. Sometimes this meant the president's house, with only a telephone number and a box number mailing address. "The only people who had their fares paid [to annual meetings] were the secretary and the president. Otherwise the individual [members] had to pay it."

The organization was formed in the 1920s. By the 1960s it appeared to be national in name only. The Maritime provinces held disproportionate representation and influence, the rest of the country seldom sending more than a few delegates to annual meetings. From 1965 to 1971, six men held the presidency. All were Maritimers, including Sam Ermen, an accountant from Moncton, and Dick Pearson, a postal employee from Saint John. The Maritime domination continued in subsequent years with Haligonians Gerry Spears, a former fight promoter also prominent in provincial baseball and softball, and Sleep (whom a disgruntled George Chuvalo nicknamed 'Murray Asleep') moving into top positions.

Dick Pearson in particular had a difficult time. Elected president in 1963, he was overwhelmed by unrelenting disparagement from across the country — and by boxing's chaotic state. He quit as president, but returned later in the decade as secretary-treasurer and a commissioner.

"The effort I was putting into the position wasn't worth the brickbats and abuse I was getting," Pearson complained to the

Canadian Press. "I felt I was doing the right thing, but I was accused by managers, promoters and other individuals of being a dictator."

Since federation officials were not paid, Pearson felt little incentive to endure the onslaught. "Boxing officials in the United States are being paid handsome salaries, but there's only abuse in Canada. I don't want to leave the game, though. I love it."

By the 1970s the Halifax Athletic Commission led the country in safety for professional boxing. Instead of the routine medicals that had been the only requirement for fighters in previous years, the commission demanded that all fighters — not just main-event fighters — undergo electroencephalograph (EEG) examinations. It also made more than a token effort to investigate and substantiate records of visiting boxers. When these two steps were diligently carried out the Halifax commission's requirements became the country's most stringent, equalled in North America only by those of the New York State Athletic Commission.

The organization attracted some of the city's most high-profile men. These included Dr. Ken Nickerson, lawyer Angus MacDonald and the ubiquitous Buddy Daye. Also among them was Gerry Spears, who was appointed commission chairman in 1969. In 1965 when he first applied for a promoter's license, Spears was shocked to learn the commission had no offices — meetings were held in the home of the secretary. When he asked to see the regulations governing promoters he was given a manual dated 1928. Even those antiquated rules were not being enforced.

"I must say that we were probably the first promoters in the Halifax area that, the day of the fight, put the purses [aside, in trust]," Spears recounted many years later. "All of this was verbal agreement, no contracts in these days. Later on when I was appointed to the commission, I felt it was my duty to draw up some rules and regulations.

"I think our commission was the first at that time to have contracts made, not only for the fighters, but for managers, seconds, referees and all officials, which had to be in the hands of the commission X number of days before the fight. And there was a tremendous amount of flak at that time from the boxers stating that we were killing boxing doing this. We felt it was better to kill boxing than to kill boxers."

While Spears was an effective administrator and a stabilizing figure, it was another man who gave the commission its highest profile, his successor Don Kerr.

Driven by an ardent competitiveness and a sense of *noblesse oblige,* Don Kerr was a great many things. Learned and patrician. Good looking and elegant. He was also a powerful Halifax attorney, a successful businessman, director of several companies, a varsity athlete and a patron of the arts, among others.

Kerr was drawn to boxing in the manner of many men of such caste — he participated in the sport when he was young. He had about 60 amateur fights, won the Nova Scotia Golden Gloves welterweight title, then had 10 professional bouts, winning most. Through the years Kerr involved himself in almost every element of the sport. He was a fight judge for many years, and later helped promote and fund the early career of Halifax-based Trevor Berbick, who in the 1980s was briefly the World Boxing Council's heavyweight champion.

While assessments of Kerr's boxing governance vary — some thought him too political, too stand-offish, or too close to some of the local characters in the sport — all recognized that he brought competitiveness and ego to his role with the local commission. He declared that under him it would be the best in the country. Most agree he succeeded. He once boasted that during his years as commission chairman no boxer entered the ring without first having an EEG and EKG.

Kerr cut a fashionable figure around town. "Kerr on the surface was definitely one of the more impressive guys," says Harris Sullivan. "Strikingly handsome, debonair. He didn't look like he belonged in boxing."

"God, that man was a sharp dresser," says Alex J. Walling. "Never saw him without his blue blazer, white shirt, red tie, white pants." He remembers too that Kerr was one of the few men who hung up on him during his morning radio show. "I called him at quarter to seven in the morning and he was totally shocked that I would call him. 'Don't you ever call me at that time!' Click! So I went on air and I said, 'I'd like to tell you about the fight, but Mr. Kerr is more interested in his beauty winks than he is about answering why we've got such a sordid mess here in boxing.' He called back. We had a little chat about that."

Promoter Sonny MacPhee calls Kerr "a fantastic man" who put interests of the fighter first and effectively settled money-related disputes. He says Kerr insisted promoters have sufficient funding — he demanded certified cheques, which he would then lock in a safe — before he'd license a fight. Still, the two men had their disagreements.

"Don used to have my ass a lot of times. [He] would always want a good card. However, I've seen him hold me up and not let me advertise because I didn't have a semi-final. I'd say, 'Don, the semi-final is the fight that comes on before the main event.' He'd say, 'No, it's got to be a special calibre fight — *a semi-final*.' I'd say, 'What page is that on?' However, he'd tell me that if it weren't strong enough, he wouldn't pass it. He was good for the game in Halifax."

Yet for some fighters, Spears and Kerr and the emphasis on the fighter's well-being emerged too late. This was painfully true in the case of a rugged lightweight named Dickie 'Kid' Howard.

Guilt-propelled charity affairs euphemistically called 'nights' channelled money to broke and desperate retired fighters sometimes too befuddled to fully understand what was happening. An example of such gloomy benevolence unfolded on the evening of June 5, 1967, when boxing fans with long memories entered the Halifax Forum to honour a man whose own memory was growing shorter by the day.

Often during Dickie 'Kid' Howard Night they rose and cheered for The Kid, just as they had risen and cheered for him round after round, fight after fight, year after year when merciful gods and Haligonian judges conspired to ensure that *his* arm was thrust skyward at ring centre.

"The Halifax Howitzer!" *A loud hum in his ears.* "The Miniature Marciano!" *Blood crusting in his nose.* "The Pocket Hercules of the Maritimes!" *His body numb.*

Many years before the city's boxing regulations were tightened, the career of Kid Howard was a cautionary tale of prizefighting's dark side. Some men were astute enough to see this side, as David Downey instinctively did, and steered his own career accordingly. Downey was determined he would not become a Kid Howard, despite the urging of old-line sportswriters. Consequently the press would never extol him in the manner it did Howard, celebrating his ability to take powerful blows, his "fathomless" determination, his courage — always Howard's courage.

No one paid The Kid much for all this. But he seldom complained. He figured the money was good enough if it kept him going until the next fight. Besides, there were other compensations to make this tiny fellow from a nearby fishing village feel he was making some progress in life. He *was* a local celebrity. His picture was in the newspaper a lot — although he couldn't read newspapers or much of anything for that matter. And frequently men with quiet lives would cheerfully buy him drinks and shake his hand and then go home and boast to their sons that they met Kid Howard today!

In the 1950s Halifax was Canada's boxing epicentre, and The Kid, Canadian lightweight champion for six years, was the main reason why. Never had anyone attracted crowds as large or as avid to the Forum. And few fighters ever benefited as much by merely being Haligonian.

"A lot of time other fighters and managers would come in here and they knew right away that it's a stacked deck," says former CBC sportscaster Gerry Fogarty. "Howard was very, very tough to knock down. [So] if he was on his feet at the end of 10 or 12 rounds, you could almost rest assured that he was going to get the decision."

The Kid weighed between 129 and 135 pounds and at five-foot-two was shorter by two, three or four inches than most opponents — many of them upper-echelon boxers. Even by the standards of the day Howard was an active fighter. Over his career he had roughly 111 professional fights, winning 77. Countless others were almost certainly unrecorded. He fought 10 times in 1950, 11 in 1951, 12 in 1952, and 10 in 1953. Over one span in 1951, long before mandatory waiting periods between fights, he fought five times in just 65 days. In 1953, it was four times in 38 days. Through it all he was never knocked out. The Kid was awfully proud of that.

"He fought all those guys that he should have never fought," says Keith Paris, who lost two decisions to Howard. "Them guys were too much for him, [they were] hittin' him on the jaw, destroyin' him. You can only take so much. [In the end] he was in bad shape, he really was. Howard just went in there and took the heat."

"One time they had him ranked eighth in the world," points out Tom McCluskey, who along with American legend Charlie Goldman trained Howard in his prime. "That was somethin' else — eighth in the world! Even at that, in reality Dickie wasn't a good fighter."

"If I had to do it all over again," Howard once told a reporter, "I would have gotten a trade. A trade means a lot. If I would have gotten a trade I don't think I would have bothered with boxing."

Following his retirement, Howard's situation was an open secret — a broken marriage, residual effects of jaundice, his daughter's death and a stay in a psychiatric hospital. Many tried to help. Often $5 bills were pressed into his palm by people he hardly knew. Acquaintances found him work, but even rudimentary tasks were arduous for a little fellow whose prizefighting wars unleashed the butterflies in his brain.

Doug Saunders, who covered boxing for CBC during the 1970s and 1980s, says the fight game turned Howard into "a vegetable" who one night during a wrestling promotion — in the ring, dressed in a suit — heard a bell ring and charged out of a corner ready to fight.

Percy Paris, who operated Halifax's Creighton Street Gym where Howard sometimes trained, recalled seeing Howard one evening in the early 1960s after he retired. "He said to me — and he didn't even know who I *was* at first — 'Can you tell me where Percy Paris' gym is at?' I fought the guy four times! I said, 'Jeez Dickie, it's right on the corner.' He said, 'Oh, I didn't know that.' "

Kid Howard Night was organized with the best of intentions by aspiring promoter Jimmy Gillis and financed by Derek Oland of

Halifax-based Oland Breweries. The program included a series of exhibition matches spotlighting old and young talent.

The occasion's feature attraction was an exhibition match scheduled for six rounds between 29-year-old George Chuvalo, Canadian heavyweight champion, and Yvon Durelle, 37, the truculent, retired light heavyweight legend. The two had fought for real in Toronto in 1959, when Chuvalo defended his Canadian heavyweight title by knocking out Durelle in 12 rounds.

Durelle, a self-confessed 'big, fat roly-poly,' prepared for the Howard exhibition by holing up for the afternoon in a Halifax tavern, then downing "a slug or two of rye" before entering the ring. Chuvalo took things much more seriously. At the opening bell he came at Durelle with unanticipated aggression, catching the older man off guard. Durelle responded, transforming a friendly sparring session into a nasty display of egos and elbows.

"It appeared to me that Chuvalo heeled Yvon in the first round and Yvon retaliated by jumping on his foot," observed Bob Edgett, a referee from New Brunswick who was at ringside. "So Chuvalo pulled an elbow, and Yvon spit in his face, a mouthful of blood, several times. There was head-butting and rabbit-punching. Both of them knew all the tricks. The end of the second round Chuvalo went back to his corner and started pounding his gloves together, and a buzz went through the crowd. 'Jeez, Chuvalo, he's going to put Yvon away, going to go all out.' And sure enough, the third round started and he charged from his corner and went at him. He had Yvon reeling, and Yvon came back and hooked Chuvalo and almost put him down."

In the fourth round, Durelle quit, exhausted.

After the fight Chuvalo's manager Irving Ungerman ventured into Durelle's dressing room to soothe matters. It didn't work. Durelle "gave him a kick in the arse" and called him "a goddamn cocksucker" and "a fuckin' bum." Ungerman left.

In the middle of the evening a short ceremony was held to present a cheque to the honouree, Kid Howard, who accepted gratefully.

Twenty-five hundred attended Kid Howard Night. Total proceeds were not announced.

7

CABARET

In the angry autumn of 1968, as the spectre of a race war loomed over Halifax, a soft-spoken middle-aged man in a working-class white neighbourhood near the Forum took delivery of a half-dozen hand guns and clandestinely began offering them to neighbours. More than one gratefully accepted. Just in case.

Imminent was the arrival of the Black Panther Party, the menacing American entity whose manifesto encouraged blacks to take up arms to resist oppression. And in the autumn of 1968 the Panthers had concluded that Halifax was an oppressed city.

Formed just two years before in Oakland, California, the Panthers renounced the integrationist, non-violent stance of Martin Luther King and rejected compromise with what it branded the 'white power structure.' Instead the Panthers championed black liberation, the emerging ideology influenced by the mesmerizing Malcolm X and others.

While it also did some public good — notably establishing clinics for sickle-cell anemia testing and introducing a free breakfast program for inner-city children — the party's prominence was almost entirely based on its propensity for confrontation and guns and its inflammatory, chilling, occasionally preposterous rhetoric. Not surprisingly the Panthers quickly became a principal target for the FBI, which successfully employed infiltration and propaganda tactics. The death or imprisonment of party leaders soon crippled the organization. In addition, bitter rivalries fomented between factions wishing to downplay violence and those favouring armed insurrection. This infighting made the Panthers even more unpredictable and volatile, never more so than in the latter part of 1968 — the period that coincided with the party's sudden interest in Halifax.

Haligonians braced themselves, their anxiety mounting with the televised images of the Watts riots that followed the assassination of Martin Luther King earlier that year.

Halifax police chief Verdun Mitchell put his force on full alert.

"I've never seen anything like the tension in this city at that time," remembers activist Joan Jones, whose then-husband Burnley 'Rocky' Jones was widely acknowledged as the leader of Halifax's more militant blacks. "I think that the white community perceived that there would be violence. Every time you turned your TV on at night you saw black people running around supposedly setting fires and being angry. And saying we are not going to take it anymore. You saw people like the Black Panthers, and you see [the] North End of Halifax which had the highest concentration of blacks at that time. What are you gonna do? Of course you're gonna get a little afraid."

That fear soared on October 16 when Stokely Carmichael touched down at Halifax International Airport. The skies could not have delivered a more adroit *provocateur*, nor anyone more central to the Panthers' inner turmoil.

Stokely Carmichael was said to be so cocky that he looked like he was strutting when he was standing still. *Life* magazine wrote that he looked like he could "stroll through Dixie in broad daylight using the Confederate flag for a handkerchief." Tall, slim and handsome, Carmichael, 37, applied splendid oratorical gifts to assail America and capitalism. He also favoured separation of the races, a view antithetical to that of King, whom Carmichael labelled an 'Uncle Tom.'

As chairman of the Student Nonviolent Co-ordinating Committee (SNCC), in 1966 he used the platform for a landmark speech at the University of California in which he called for "black power." The phrase galvanized young blacks, alarmed white America and annoyed SNCC leaders, who demanded Carmichael calm his tone. He refused. So in 1967 the organization severed all ties with him. Almost immediately he joined the Panthers and was appointed honorary prime minister.

But Carmichael quickly found that even the Black Panther Party was not radical enough, and he raged against its "ill-prepared leadership" and "dogmatic party line favoring alliances with white radicals."

By the time of his Halifax visit Carmichael almost certainly realized his time as a Panther was nearing an end, one way or another. So he almost always travelled with bodyguards, mindful of more than just *white* assassins.

Carmichael had met Rocky Jones a short time before in Montreal at a highly charged writers' conference where Carmichael impelled Canadian blacks to "get all the guns you can and be prepared to kill for your people." The language infuriated many Canadians (former prime minister John Diefenbaker labelled Carmichael "revolutionary riff-raff") but it intrigued Jones. The two spent a lot of time together. "We just clicked. There was something about his energy and my energy — there was a synergy. We were able to talk about everything. We could see things almost through the same lens. Stokely was a very brilliant person. He liked head games — a lot of intellectual exercise. Very passionate in what he believed in, and very brave how he confronted it. And yet, he was a nice guy to sit back [with] and have a drink and talk."

Jones invited him to Nova Scotia to 'chill' for a few days. No one was to know. Carmichael accepted, but the plan never had a chance. "I didn't know how closely we were monitored. The cops knew every move we were making. We arrived at the airport there's all of these policemen! Holy shit! It was unbelievable. I wasn't expecting it."

Carmichael commuted from the airport to North Preston, a black community outside Dartmouth then known locally for its high crime rate and dirt roads. There he spoke to schoolchildren and mingled with other groups, all under the gaze of several plainclothes cops. One of his longest stops during his trip was at the

Arrows Club, the North End night spot owned by Billy Downey, one of David's older brothers.

A stocky, bearded railway porter in his late 30s, Billy Downey was a competent professional boxer in the early 1950s. But an entrepreneurial spirit and outgoing personality drove a dream of opening his own nightclub. Making it happen required incalculable vigilance along with various business and political connections, as well as a good deal of help from other Downeys, especially brother Graham, who became Billy's partner in the project. David also pitched in, doing tasks such as standing at the door, counting cash and tending the bar.

It would be a memorable night at the club for all three brothers.

Earlier that day someone had phoned Graham and asked if the club would host the Trinidad-born Carmichael and others for a meal of black-eyed peas, sweet potato, honey and rice — a West Indian favourite that happened to be an Arrows speciality thanks to the club's long-time cook, a sharp-dressed middle-aged woman named Zena Williams.

Carmichael arrived late in the afternoon. "I can remember looking out on the street and seeing [the police] motorcade, how it pulled up with the lights going, and how he got out and walked in," says Graham Downey. Carmichael was joined by roughly a dozen others including Rocky and Joan Jones, Buddy Daye, university professor George McCurdy and Carmichael's wife, the singer Miriam Makeba. The large group immediately repaired to an upstairs meeting room. Police surrounded the club, elevating local apprehension and Graham's blood pressure. He called David for some support. When the fighter arrived he spotted several police sharpshooters on a rooftop nearby, their rifles in full view. "Are they crazy?" he remembers thinking.

At 9 pm Billy Downey pulled up in a taxi. Just ending his railway shift on *The Scotian*, Downey blinked as he peered out the cab window. "Jesus! Look at the cops! There must be a big fight in the club tonight!"

"Not a fight, Billy," the cabbie relayed. "Stokely Carmichael's in town. He's got 'em all shook up."

Downey hopped out of the cab. David greeted him.

"Billy, we got a lot of company here," said the boxer, "Look right up there behind you."

Billy twisted around and looked up at the police snipers. "Holy shit," he said.

He quickly approached police Sergeant Bill MacDonald, whom he knew. "Jesus Christ, Billy, I'm glad you got in town," said the cop.

"What's the matter?"

"Stokely Carmichael's in there! Rocky Jones and them guys, they're in there talkin' black power! You know we don't bother you guys ...."

Billy hurried inside and found Graham, who explained about the request and the meeting and the black-eyed peas. Billy returned to MacDonald. "Sergeant, you wanna come in?" He did not.

Billy re-entered the club. Upstairs he introduced himself to Carmichael and Makeba. He was charmed by the singer, whose entrée to mainstream culture was the whimsical hit song *The Bucket Gotta Hole In It*, which she performed with Harry Belafonte. He then asked Makeba to go downstairs and do a number with the week's featured performer, Lottsa Poppa (a.k.a. Four Hundred Pounds of Soul).

Makeba hesitated. Carmichael did not.

"We don't sit with white people," said the Panther. "The only way — the *only* way — we go downstairs is if you separate *us* from *them*."

Billy, who at the time was dating a white woman, glared at Carmichael. "We just can't do that, Stokely. You can come down and watch the show. We'll be honoured. But we can't segregate the club like that. Whites on one side, blacks on the other. That's not our game."

Billy calmly listened to Carmichael's surly disapproval then offered a compromise. "What we *can* do, we can go down and make a space for you. But we can't segregate the club. If people come in, they gotta be able to sit wherever they can get a seat. You may be sittin' alongside of a white person. I just can't segregate the club like that."

Carmichael finally relented. Downey roped off a section of the club for the group, then bought drinks for the whole party. The mood improved further when Makeba strode on stage to do a number with Lottsa Poppa. Then a second song. Then another. Forty minutes later she and Four Hundred Pounds of Soul finished to the wild appreciation of the racially mixed crowd.

"We tried to keep them to themselves, if they wanted to, but we wouldn't break up our tables or nothin' like that," says Billy today. "And them guys got up and danced with the white girls! Rocky Jones danced with a white girl too."

At some point in the night Carmichael even agreed to an interview with a young radio reporter from Dartmouth station CFDR. About 3 am the group departed the Arrows.

"The next morning," says Billy, "we went home and all over the airwaves they were blastin' Stokely Carmichael was at the Arrows Club on the corner of West and Agricola and they are organizing to come back here — the Black Panthers — and what they were gonna do. But that wasn't the real story at all."

Late that morning Carmichael left the city, his northern visit lasting just 18 hours and invigorating some local black leaders, but bringing no violence. Nonetheless, his parting words at the airport granted Haligonians no comfort. He told the *Chronicle-Herald,* "We recognize all the problems of Halifax that black people have, and we wanted to begin some co-ordination so that we can move against racism and capitalism."

(About a week after Stokely Carmichael departed Halifax, and 13 months after the frenzied episode on Gottingen Street during which he stood above the pandemonium and emerged a civic hero, Halifax police chief Verdun Mitchell tragically took his own life. Twenty-five hundred attended his funeral.)

In mid-November four more Black Panthers arrived in town. One was Canadian, three were American. They did not come as tourists.

Prominent among their activities were two important, blacks-only meetings. The first took place at the Cornwallis Street Baptist Church. At the church arrangements were made and an agenda set for another meeting — an all-black "family" meeting — the following week, at the North End Library.

Before it began, the library meeting was confronted with the predicament of white spouses, who insisted they were true "family" and therefore had a right to sit in. "It might not have been an issue in Mississippi," smiles Rocky Jones today, "but it was certainly an issue here." In the end, whites were not permitted to attend.

Four hundred attended *in camera*, many associated with black organizations from around the area. The meeting's most significant outcome was the formation of the Black United Front (BUF), an 'umbrella' for black groups such as the Nova Scotia Association for the Advancement of Coloured People and the African Baptists Association. BUF's *raison d'être* was to find a common purpose for Nova Scotia blacks, achieve greater dignity within the black community and make economic and political inroads. Its executive was quick to assure the media that BUF was not a Panther affiliate.

Still, city authorities remained uneasy about this new body, possessing the ominous name but replete with figures not known to be radicals. These included three members of the Oliver family. Dr. William Pearly Oliver, a Baptist minister and provincial government employee working in adult education, was appointed BUF chairman. His son Jules was executive director, and brother Donald a director. The fear was that rejecting the organization could propel militant factions to seize control of BUF. This, in turn, could trigger untold consequences. Not the least of these was the disruption of the first Canada Summer Games, scheduled for next August, which both the city and the province were counting on to showcase a new, modern Halifax to the rest of the country. So government money flowed to BUF — more than $500,000 over its first five years. It was enough to keep the militants at bay.

When the all-black meeting at the library adjourned, Canadian Panther Roosevelt 'Rosie' Douglas, a McGill University student, walked up the street and began talking with some young blacks outside the Creighton Street Gym. Four times Halifax police asked Douglas to move along. Finally he was arrested for loitering.

Ordinarily it would have been a minor incident, but in the fall of 1968 it became a *cause célèbre*.

In court Douglas refused to pay a $5 fine and chose instead to spend five days in jail. However, after a five-hour discussion with deputy police chief John Wrin, Douglas's fine was paid. A short time later the two men appeared together at a late-night press conference. Wrin extended his hand to Douglas. The Panther turned away.

Around the same time another Panther-related drama was unfolding. It involved a man soon to become one of the most infamous of all party members, George Sams Jr.

Shortly after the all-black meeting, Sams — who arrived in Halifax under the alias of Robert Waddell Smith — was stopped by police for a minor traffic violation while driving Rocky Jones's Volkswagen. When police searched the car they found an unloaded .38-calibre revolver under the front passenger seat and three rifles elsewhere in the car. The latter were explained away through Jones being an avid duck hunter. Today Jones is confident that the revolver was planted earlier that day, when the car was parked in his driveway, by a black associate — formerly his bodyguard. Sams was fined $50 for illegal firearm possession, then taken into custody by Canadian immigration officials and subsequently deported. His lawyer was Donald Oliver, now a Canadian senator. It is unlikely Oliver realized the true nature of his client.

George Sams snickered at his nicknames 'Crazy George' and 'The Madman.' He found 'psychopath' less amusing. But it was just as accurate.

The stocky, powerfully built, 24-year-old native of Detroit was once described by fellow Panther Frances Carter as "the biggest fool, the ugliest bastard I'd ever seen. Talking crazy, his eyes deep, beet red. Just stunk like 10 dogs. Foamy when he talked. Almost like a Halloween character. Scary! He was sick, sexually perverted, always trying to work his will and wanting to forcibly have sex. He was the kiss of death."

Sams spent much of his youth in a New York institution for 'mental defectives,' and much of his young adulthood in jails. A bullet fragment in his head was a souvenir of a failed armed robbery in Detroit in 1964. His body contained seven bullet holes in all. Rumours alleged he punched pregnant women and once threatened to have his own mother killed. Rocky Jones recalls that Sams liked to suck his thumb.

Sams' most notorious act was to take place in the late spring of 1969, six months after his truncated visit to Halifax.

Claiming he was assigned by the Panther central committee, Sams led a one-man reign of terror at the party's New Haven chapter. There he helped kill a young Panther named Alex Rackley, whom Sams said was a police informant. Before Rackley was shot, Sams tortured him for three days at a local Panthers' house, stabbing him with an ice pick, refusing him regular toilet privileges and ordering boiling water poured on his skin. An autopsy showed severe burns on wide areas of his buttocks, thighs, chest, wrists and right shoulder. Rackley was also beaten with a hard object around the groin, face and back.

Despite his deep involvement in the crime, during the murder trial Sams appeared as the 'star' witness for the *government* and was given a light sentence.

On December 6, with the arrests of Sams and Douglas dominating the news, a day-and-a-half public assembly called the Human Rights Conference opened at a North End school — a location strategically selected for its slum surroundings. Its theme was *The Black Man in Nova Scotia.* The conference proved a tangled mixture of good intentions, expert oratory and political clumsiness.

It opened with 700 people on hand — about two-thirds of them white, an army of plainclothes cops moving among them. Its overarching goal was to urge Nova Scotian blacks to discover their own solutions and select their own leaders with minimal white involvement.

Two speakers, both black, calmed the mood. Howard McCurdy, a dapper 35-year-old microbiologist from the University of Windsor, pulled back from the Panther rhetoric thundering across the city. "We cannot blame all of our problems on white people," he said. "Those who use black power as a new kind of racism must be disavowed." John Cartwright, of Boston University, termed black power a defensive response to external forces, but discouraged the use of violence.

Sandwiched between McCurdy and Cartwright was Nova Scotia Premier G. I. Smith, a 57-year-old lawyer who arrived brandishing a letter he had received from a local black group. The letter outlined 28 points to improve the conditions of blacks in the province. Smith addressed all 28 points, promising along the way a housing program, more black school teachers, road improvement, tighter scrutiny of hiring practices, new housing legislation and better enforcement of the provincial human rights act.

And then a final promise.

Smith proudly said he was forming a new office — Director of Human Rights for Nova Scotia. He announced its first director, Marvin Schiff, who was seated in the audience. Schiff stood. Several people in the audience gasped. Schiff was white.

A 31-year-old Jew from Toronto, his qualifications for the $16,000-a-year job were highlighted thus: he had studied social work at the University of Windsor, travelled in the Middle East and Africa, and worked the social science beat for the *Globe and Mail*. Grilled by the audience as to why a Halifax black was not given the job, a government official explained that none of the seven black applicants was qualified. Many left the meeting stunned.

In spite of this initial reaction, after a few months in the office Schiff was drawing cautious endorsements. One of the more interesting came from Donald Oliver who reasoned that as a Jew, Schiff could empathize and therefore do "better than an ordinary WASP." Schiff would hold the post for three years, until he was replaced in 1971 by Dr. George McCurdy, a black man from Amherstburg, Ontario.

The jumbled bid by the Panthers to Americanize the local racial quandary did not succeed. Canada's civil rights movement was a child of the peace movement and therefore possessed neither the stridency nor the urgency of the American effort. Walter Fitzgerald, then a Halifax alderman, recalls, "There was a lot of tension when they came to town because we didn't know what they were going to do, how much support they'd get. But I don't think the local [black] population were that impressed with them."

For years Rocky Jones was a prime target in RCMP undercover investigations — the Jones family telephone would shut off mysteriously during the night, their mail would arrive in a bundle about once a week instead of daily and plainclothes cops would follow Rocky everywhere. Aware of the often-clumsy scrutiny, he sometimes teased his shadows. He once invited a Mountie into his house for a game of cards.

But for those connected with the Panthers' visit and other civil rights events during the era there was additional drama, of a more personal kind. The home of Rocky and Joan Jones drew special attention.

"We would get death threats and a lot of times it really appeared dangerous," remembers Joan. "When someone calls you and tells you that they are a member of the Klan, what are you going to do?"

In the face of this threat, Panther types — "the big Afro, the beret, the jackets, the whole thing" — would walk their daughters to school, Joan Jones recalls. "Imagine what it would look like with a little six-year-old skipping in between [these guys. My daughter] remembers that because it was so much fun. Those people were gentle and kind to her, and she always had an arm to hold."

The couple was determined their children would live normally during the turmoil, and they did. "It was hard because we had meetings all the time in our house," says Rocky. "We always stressed co-operation and family values. And anyone who came in our house had to abide by that."

Says Joan, "My house was always full. People were always coming and going. Life was an adventure every single day. [I'd] speak at the Lions Club, at the Rotary Club, at the Y, at the Boys Scouts, and it takes a while to realize you are just the flavour of the month. At the universities, y'know, the more you would insult these people the harder they would clap. We'd go home and laugh and say, 'That's kinda weird.' "

For the police, especially the RCMP, the period was a nightmare. Fearing the Panthers would incite riots, the Mounties spied on almost everyone connected with the local civil rights movement. They scrutinized airports and the U.S.-Canada border, copied notes from university bulletin boards, went undercover into black nightclubs, infiltrated all-black meetings and cultivated informants. The racial stereotypes found in their copious files compiled over those years stunned everyone when the documents were made public in the mid-1990s. Black women were depicted as "prolific child-bearers" and black men as layabouts, thieves and drunks who "work long enough to make money for another liquor binge."

William Higgit, the future RCMP commissioner, and then national director of security and intelligence, wrote a secret report to government in December 1968, following the human rights conference. "US Black Panther members have been actively engaged in attempts to gain control of civil rights leadership in the Halifax and area Negro community," it said. "Their presence has created wide publicity and a psychological effect on the normally docile coloured population that could easily develop into an explosive situation."

Wrote one RCMP constable, "Although the Black Panther movement is gaining ground, their disciples consist mainly of the illiterate, semi-literate and hoodlums. There are a few coloured youths in this area who like to think of themselves as Black Panthers. This group, at the most 10 people, occasionally rolls drunks, etc. I suppose they feel it is more flattering to be referred to as Panthers than as thieves."

David Downey would have little overt involvement with local civil right activities, despite the fact that no Nova Scotian black athlete at the time was in a better position to contribute. His good looks, elevated profile (especially in the North End) and gregarious personality all could have been useful. But while in the United States star athletes such as Muhammad Ali and Olympic sprinters Tommie Smith and John Carlos lent their influence to the cause, in Nova Scotia Downey felt no similar sense of burden.

If he was aware of the deep and intricate frustrations all around him, his actions did not reflect this. Hardly a racial ideologue, he aligned with neither the moderate nor the militant.

Vince Hennebury, Murray Langford and David Downey greet a young fan.

However, Downey was courted. When approached by Rocky Jones, he recalls being direct. "I don't want to be mixed up in this. Nobody's botherin' me. I can't see anybody sitting up here and arguing for foolishness. What do we do? You got Dr. Martin Luther King trying to straighten this thing out, and the way you guys are talking now, you want to start somethin' like a war? We don't need this."

Certainly Jones felt there could have been a role for him, but he understood Downey's choice to be moderate. However, he feels the boxer did advance the cause of the black community, albeit in his own way. "He carried himself at all times like a gentleman, as a role model."

The Black United Front also had plans for Downey. It asked him to be a youth counsellor, presented him with a gold pin and invited him to meetings. Downey attended a few, but backed away when the organization's executive started to change.

Downey also interacted with Buddy Daye, but found his intricate networking of disparate factions confusing.

Suspicious of a process he had little stomach for in the first place, Downey ultimately resisted the activists as effectively as he had resisted boxing promoters and sportswriters, intuitively wary of playing a dupe for anyone or any organization. "Nobody was gonna tell me something to get me in trouble. I was tryin' to build up a name."

Against this capricious backdrop Downey's prizefighting career moved into its most active period. Twenty-seven days after dispensing with Stu Gray, Downey fought to a draw against a gangly American who had not had a match in three years, Don Turner.

Decades later, Turner would become one of boxing's best trainers, in association with welterweight Aaron Pryor, heavyweight Evander Holyfield and a galaxy of other champions. This success would come at the end of a long, rough road that began in the Cincinnati projects with a childhood he often described as "a three-meals-a-day upbringing: missed meals, no meals and oatmeal." He learned to fight to keep bullies from stealing his lunch money, and in the process realized a valuable lesson in life: Pain gives respect.

Turner was an undistinguished professional fighter who earned pitiable purses — once just $80 for a 10-round bout — and lived frugally. He once sat in an Atlantic City movie theatre and watched Elvis Presley's *Viva Las Vegas* four times because he couldn't afford a hotel room. He then got up, strolled across the street and won a match, pocketing $250. For facing Downey, Rocco Jones paid him about $1,000.

Although he suffered the fight's only cut, Turner felt he beat Downey. He was not alone. Fans in the Halifax Forum jeered the announcement of a draw. The *Chronicle-Herald* called the decision "controversial."

Tom McCluskey had devised Downey's fight plan and worked in his corner. "Christ almighty! Dave was so friggin' scared that night. [He] was scared shitless of the guy. I had Dave goin' like a rabbit that night. I knew what you had to do to survive, right? So he got the fight in and looked pretty good doin' it."

Many years later Turner told McCluskey he thought he was robbed that night, though he added that Downey was a "*good* little boxer."

Five weeks later Downey was in another Rocco Jones promotion, this time in the Fairview Centennial Arena, an unadorned and damp hockey rink in a Halifax suburb with a flourishing dope trade and dowdy apartments. The foe was Valley Valasquez, an American journeyman. Valasquez was obscure enough to be omitted from *The Ring Record Book and Boxing Encyclopedia*, and noteworthy primarily because of his manager, a blubbery Runyonesque creature named 'Two-Ton' Tony Galento, a second-rate movie actor and 1940s heavyweight contender once knocked out by Joe Louis.

A small crowd witnessed a wacky display that saw Downey register a third-round knockout after Valasquez leapt out of the ring and refused to return. "They counted him out outside the ring. He was standin' there lookin' at me! [He] said I was a crazy man. The referee was calling him in," laughs Downey.

Downey–Valasquez was another financial flop for Jones, who had convinced his old friend Percy Paris to co-promote the card. Paris lost between $3,000 and $4,000 in the deal.

Sustaining a brisk pace, just 22 days later in Edmonton, Downey brushed aside a respectable boxer-puncher from Winnipeg named Ray Christianson. The card also featured Edmonton slugger Johan Louw, a transplanted South African who had won his first seven fights, six by knockout. Just 1,800 spectators turned up.

The promotion was little more than a transparent prerequisite for a Downey–Louw showdown. Indeed Downey–Louw could have promoted itself: a black Canadian champion — albeit one with a cautious distance between himself and the black movement — against a white South African in the heyday of apartheid. Canadian sportswriters either missed the point or shied away from it. Downey told the *Edmonton Journal* he might fight Louw early in the new year, perhaps in Edmonton. But he cautioned that his plans first called for a match with New York native Carlos Mark, a slick, former top-10 fighter. The battle was scheduled for the fall in Halifax. "It'll be a real fight for me. It means a lot. If I can beat Mark, it would jump me right up into the world rankings, 15th or 10th. A victory against Mark is the break I need. Age is creeping up on me."

Unfortunately for Downey the break turned out to be a bad one. Mark knocked heads with a sparring partner during training and pulled out of the match. The missed opportunity was possibly the most consequential twist in Downey's career. Instead of the highly regarded Mark, in November he faced another New Yorker, Dave Dittmar — an opponent the *Chronicle-Herald* at various times in its advance coverage called 'Pitmore,' 'Pitmar,' 'Ditmore' and 'Dittmare.'

Dittmar's main tactic against Downey was to crouch low, crouch often. It didn't help much. Downey knocked him out in the ninth round and today scarcely even remembers the fight.

Promoter Rocco Jones wishes he could have forgotten it, too. Downey–Dittmar drew just 760 fans.

In early January 1970 Jones signed Downey to face Freddie Martinovich. A 26-year-old Hungarian southpaw from New Jersey, Martinovich was co-managed by New York veteran Sam McGee and 'Two-Ton' Tony Galento, who four months before had delivered to Halifax the highly evasive Valley Valasquez.

A natural welterweight in his second middleweight fight, Martinovich boasted he'd never been off his feet — an intriguing claim given that he had at least nine losses on his record. To protect his man against Downey, who had developed into a large middleweight, Galento shrewdly had the contract stipulate that Martinovich would weigh 156 pounds. Downey could weigh no more than 158. The clause would prove significant. Downey failed to make weight, coming in at 164. He blamed his extra girth on the Forum's scales and even brought out his own bathroom scales at a second weigh-in to underscore their deficiency. The card was cancelled.

"Downey claims he got a raw deal," wrote *Chronicle-Herald* columnist Maurice MacDonald. "If he had been in shape there would be no 'raw deal.' The matter is clear-cut. He didn't live up to the terms of his contract. The promoters were hurt, the fans were hurt, but most of all boxing was hurt. And in its vulnerable position, injuries of this sort could be fatal to the sport."

8

BOMBER

Downey's next opponent could easily have been someone *other* than Gary Broughton. "It could have been a guy from Vancouver," says Rocco Jones, "but we picked a guy from Ontario — lighter on the transportation, y'know."

As he prepared to contest David Downey for the Canadian middleweight championship in December 1970, Gary Broughton had 13 wins, 19 losses and three draws. Despite this feeble resume his calendar was usually full and the span between appointments rarely exceeded a couple of months. Promoters would happily overlook unremarkable records for fighters like him, whose bouts possessed grit, strain and a warrior's honour. Broughton revelled in the brutal, honest sweat of his profession. All the better if his opponent shared the inclination. "Win or lose, the fans knew they had seen a real scrap," he once boasted.

"I wasn't sweet, smooth like silk. But I could box and I could block — block with my hands and block with my shoulders. And I could hit. That put me in a very good position because I could be losing a boxing match and suddenly catch a guy with a knock and knock him dizzy."

Ted Beare, retired sports editor of the *Brantford Expositor*, says Broughton would take on all comers, the hell with their record. "He'd stand there and they'd knock him around and he didn't care. But he got in his shots, too. He more or less took on the philosophy that, hey, whoever is left standing at the end, well, he wins."

"I hesitate to say that they were all wars," says Ron Craig, a friend of Broughton's, "but he could *make* them into wars. That's the way he fought. He didn't take any prisoners."

Gary Broughton was not a common pug, although he presented the stock features. Born in England, raised near Kitchener, Ontario, he had a lean, angular body that appeared taller than its actual five-foot-eight. A receding hairline exposed a resilient white face that bore a flat, battered nose and other vocational inscriptions of which he seemed not at all concerned. His natural countenance bordered on a pout, but his smile could bloom with childlike impishness. In both accent and attitude he retained his middle-class British roots, and was easily moved to discussions on history, philosophy and current events.

After failed stabs at other high school sports, Broughton began to train in a local gym. His amateur matches took place at the near-by Galt Legion facility. As he waited to go into the ring before his third fight, a man he did not recognize approached him in his dressing room. The stranger stepped close and calmly offered advice about Broughton's opponent. *"He drops his left hand after throwing a jab. Let him hit you, watch his hand drop, then throw an overhand right — directly on the chin — he'll go down."*

The stranger then walked away.

"Sure enough," recalls Broughton, "the guy did it. And — wham! I knocked him down."

The stranger was Frank Bricker, from Brantford, Ontario.

Seventy miles west of Toronto, nestled along Grand River, Brantford in the 1960s was a thoroughly ordinary Canadian municipality. Its extended population of 35,000 whites and 9,000 natives coexisted more or less in harmony, save for some boozy weekend quarrels on Market Street and other minor incidents. Brantford defined itself mainly through the manufacture of farm equipment and a short list of celebrities led by telephone inventor Alexander Graham Bell and early television actor Jay Silverheels.

Manager Frank Bricker and his protegé Gary Broughton (c. 1962).

Sports also helped sculpt Brantford's self-image. Baseball, lacrosse and hockey were popular. Boxing was Brantford's sports paradox. While the town rarely hosted major fight cards, it spawned myriad amateur and professional champions. Many of those accomplished boxers — among them Gordie Wallace, a British Empire light heavyweight champion in the 1950s — attributed their success to Frank Bricker, a Massey Ferguson foreman and ex-fighter.

Broughton and Bricker would be together for 20 years — in effect, Broughton's entire boxing career. From the beginning Bricker knew that in Broughton he had a protege of crude natural ability who would train hard and follow instructions. In Bricker, Broughton had an emotional rudder and seasoned manager whom he respected and liked. "Frank was like my brother — my big brother in boxing. He was my guardian angel. He protected me. He protected all the kids. It's hard to explain. He had an *essence* that he was protective. [At] the same time, he was tough. It was tough love. It wasn't namby-pamby. You'd do as he told ya."

Ted Beare noted Bricker's protective instincts. "He certainly wouldn't have taken the kind of cut [a manager] in New York would have taken. I don't remember one good fighter who ever left Bricker. He was his own man and his fighters were *his* fighters."

Bricker's 'Legion 90' gym was a makeshift facility on the third floor of the local Branch 90 Royal Canadian Legion Hall. It was open to anyone willing to show respect for the craft, including local youngsters from poor and broken homes whom Bricker counselled — whether or not they showed boxing potential. But while the voice was soft and the eyes fraternal, Bricker suffered no fools. Says George Garvey, of Brantford, who trained under Bricker, "Other clubs in Ontario would say, 'You're from Brantford! They train their fighters by bangin' their heads off the wall.' We fought harder in the gym sometimes than we'd ever fight in a ring. It was sort of like go in, take a punch, then give three or four back."

Broughton's amateur phase started in 1960 and lasted four-and-a-half years. Most of his 31 amateur bouts were victories. In 1964 he won the Buffalo Golden Gloves championship, then turned professional. He won his first two pro fights by knockout and swiftly earned the tag 'Brantford Bomber.' However, as his pugilistic limitations were exposed his record sank. By the end of 1969 he was 11–18 with three draws. The losses were often to quicker, more experienced Americans, although none were tougher than Broughton, whose philosophy held that wars are not won by fleeing from the enemy.

Win or lose, Broughton remained resolute. "Boxing is the only thing that's ever brought me a sense of accomplishment," he explained to the *Kitchener-Waterloo Record*. "And now boxing is so much a part of my life I'll never leave it."

Broughton was barely known in Halifax. Prior to facing Downey for the first time, in September 1970, he had never fought in the Maritimes. He was a mystery even to promoter Rocco Jones. "He was hustlin' for money. I don't think he was getting the fights that he should have. He was just good enough that some other fighters were staying away from him. The other managers seen how good he was. And David didn't know how good he was."

In an era before matches were routinely taped and copies widely available, fighters learned second- or third-hand of an opponent's style and tendencies. The only common opponent of Downey and Broughton was Stu Gray, whom Downey knocked out in eight rounds in his only previous title defence, and whom Broughton beat twice in 1969, in fights just 24 days apart.

In his most recent bout, in early July, Downey had bulked up and handily defeated light heavyweight Freddie Williams. Broughton's tune-up was less impressive — a split decision in Windsor, Ontario over Primus Williams, a 31-year-old Cincinnati club fighter who scratched Broughton under his left eye and drove a couple of Broughton's own teeth through his lower lip, sending blood gushing onto his chest. For this the Brantford Bomber earned $150 and Williams' regard. "I like any fighter with guts, and he's got guts."

On a humid September evening, six days before he was due to fight for the Canadian middleweight championship, Gary Broughton sat scoffing beer in a Brantford pub where he had become a regular. At his table was his friend Tom Conway, an industrious young sports columnist for the *Kitchener-Waterloo Record.* In previous columns Conway had taken up Broughton's cause and written that Downey — whom he termed 'an East Coast Negro'—was avoiding the Brantford Bomber. As Broughton talked and Conway scribbled, another patron shuffled up to their table.

"Hey, aren't you fightin' for the championship soon? Whatya doin' drinkin' beer?"

Broughton pivoted in his chair and glared at the interloper.

"*You* don't know the first bloody thing about it!" he snorted. "So don't ask stupid questions!"

There were no further questions.

"These guys make me laugh," Broughton crabbed to Conway as the man moved away. "They're all experts. They don't know what the hell they are talking about. Do you know what I weigh now? A hundred and fifty-one. That Downey's going to come in at 160 or more. I need a few beers to put some weight on. Anyway, I'll sweat it out of me tomorrow morning."

Broughton grinned and raised his glass. "Yes, this is my last chance to relax. From now on, it's all business."

Meanwhile in Halifax, to publicize his title defence, Downey agreed to be introduced to spectators at a professional wrestling card at the Forum. As the ring announcer began, the champion stood in one corner of the ring, awaiting his cue to skip to the centre and accept encouragement from 4,000 patrons.

"And now ladies and gentlemen, this Thursday night, right here at the Forum ... he will be defending his Canadian middleweight championship against top contender Gary Broughton from Brantford, Ontario.

"Ladies and gentlemen, please welcome the middleweight champion of Canada ....

"A big hand for ....

"Halifax's own ... um ...."

Downey froze. His face strained into a grin while awkward seconds passed as the announcer laboured to remember the name.

Finally, someone in the crowd shouted "Dave Downey!"

Downey ambled forward and waved. But the incident hurt. He left the Forum immediately.

"I'm the champ and they don't even remember my name in my home town," he later moaned.

Broughton arrived in Halifax early in the week of the fight, accompanied by May and Frank Bricker and a cocksure attitude. The trio had travelled in the manager's Ford sedan all the way from Brantford — a 30-hour expedition punctuated by a one-night stay in a motel. For much of the journey the fighter snoozed in the back seat. It was just as well he did. "When we got down there that day there was no place to room," remembers May Bricker. "I guess Rocco was supposed to get us a room — they usually do. But there was a big convention and there wasn't a thing to rent. And we couldn't get a hold of Rocco. He was 'unavailable.' "

They eventually secured a couple of rooms in an unassuming

house owned by a widow, who took a liking to the Brickers, even teaching May how to make homemade wine.

Within hours of arriving, Broughton had harnessed the local media and was spouting the usual cant when Bricker pried his fighter away to meet Tom McCluskey, whom Bricker had asked to assist in Broughton's corner. It was an astute move that would shape the fight, as well as its frenzied aftermath.

Few men inhabit the orthodoxy of prizefighting more comfortably than Tom McCluskey, Halifax's version of Hollywood's crusty sage, direct from central casting, whose sandpaper growl rationalizes boxing and life.

"I did what I did for hardly anything," he reflects on his half-century of tutoring Maritime prizefighters. "It was for the love of it. Why should I sit and cry about it now? What I did, I did to try and prove what I am. I didn't only want the fellow that I was workin' with to win, I wanted someone to say, 'Jeez, that Tom McCluskey is a good fight man.' "

McCluskey was born on Prince Edward Island in 1924 and served as a petty officer aboard corvettes during the Second World War. Boxing was in his genes. His father Bernie was a fighter, as was his uncle Tom "Oneman" McCluskey, a lumberjack from Maine who was state heavyweight champion in the Jack Johnson era, when blacks seldom fought whites. One of his brothers, Wilfred, is a respected boxing writer. Two other brothers, Ace and Cobey, were accomplished middleweights, both Maritime champions. Cobey fought Yvon Durelle in three wild matches in the early 1950s. Tom had only moderate success as a welterweight active throughout the Maritimes and New England. "I wasn't a good fighter. I'm a trainer and a fight man. I know greatness when it's there and when it's not there."

McCluskey was employed by the Department of National Defence for nearly 40 years, finding time at night and on days off to pursue his passion. Over the years he aided a very credible cast of local fighters, including Buddy Daye, Archie Lee, Les Sprague, Les Gillis, Dickie Howard, Keith Paris, Blair Richardson, Ralph Hollett, Trevor Berbick and the Hafey brothers. He also promoted some fight cards on Prince Edward Island.

McCluskey excelled with boxers who had heart, men unafraid to plumb the depths of effort and valour. "Management means nothin'. If you have the heart, the guts, the skill, the chin, the punch, and it's in your blood, and you are born to be a champion just like a race horse, if you have that blood stream runnin' through ya, God and high water are not gonna stop ya."

Halifax's sportswriters were fond of McCluskey. He made good copy and his demeanour emitted credibility.

"I always liked him," says Harris Sullivan. "[He] devoted a lot of time to the sport. I always had the impression that he knew what he was doing. He knew how to handle fighters."

"I'd put him up there with the best trainers ever," asserts Doug Saunders. "I wouldn't give him a back seat to any trainer in North America. I've seen McCluskey take guys with no talent and make them into Canadian champions. Look at Ralph Hollett. [But] if he doesn't like a boxer, for whatever reasons — be it style or a personal conflict with the man — you're never gonna change his mind. He's gonna change yours. And he is goddamned convincing."

McCluskey, then in his mid-40s, would be Broughton's operative for his first contest with Downey. Previously he had trained the Halifax fighter and worked in his corner for a few fights. In the process McCluskey had effectively *absorbed* Downey, studying his inclinations during combat, attending his final thoughts in the dressing room, and at decisive moments peering into his eyes and seeing his heart.

"[Downey] was a good, clean-cut guy and he could box quite well, [but] he would not go to extremes. He would not go another step forward [the way] some fighters would [and say] 'I don't think I can beat this guy but I'll fight him anyway, I'll give him everything I got.' Downey wasn't that type."

Downey and McCluskey enjoyed a mostly pleasant relationship. McCluskey says the low point with Downey and his associates would invariably arrive when it was time to be paid for his services. By the early 1970s this problem had driven McCluskey away from Downey.

"I said I don't go that route anymore. So Broughton came to town, right? I worked Broughton's corner."

Downey denies shortchanging McCluskey or anyone else who helped him. Moreover, even today he still feels that McCluskey was disloyal to assist his opponents. "They could have gotten anybody in the Forum that night to work in Broughton's corner. Someone said Tom volunteered. Even him volunteering — you don't do that. No matter a white or a black fighter or what. Here you are going against me. [I] don't think no other top trainer would do that."

McCluskey knew little about Broughton professionally and nothing about him personally. That would change.

"All that I've got in my mind — I'm so fight crazy — is that I want Broughton to beat Downey. No in-between, I wanted him to beat Downey."

At their first meeting McCluskey took one look at Broughton and formed his impression. *"He's a bum,"* McCluskey silently concluded. *"A punchin' bag. Fight anybody, anytime, any place — if the money's right."* He also surmised Broughton did not have a viable fight plan for the mobile Downey.

McCluskey stared at the fighter. "If I'm gonna be involved in this—and it looks like I am—then we're gonna win. If you're here and pussyfoot around and think you are gonna go in there and come out with a nice little decision, you're crazy. Downey can box, he can move on his feet, he's got legs. If you're gonna go that route, then you're gonna be a loser before you leave the dressing room."

McCluskey paused to inspect the reactions of Broughton and Bricker. "What do you people have in mind?"

"You seem to know what you're talkin' about," Bricker offered.

"I *do* know what I'm talkin' about."

"What d'you say then?" Bricker asked.

"I say when the bell rings he goes out and meets this nice clean-cut kid head-to-head and takes every bit of fight that's in him, out of him. Within how many rounds he can do it? I don't know. But he's got to take the fight right away from him. Forget about what he can do, what he can't do, that he can jab, he can move, he can box — throw all that out the window."

McCluskey paused again. "Who's gonna be the toughest guy here? Who can take the most? Who can give the most? That's who's gonna win."

He then looked back at Broughton. "Where are you comin' from?"

"That's the way I fight," Broughton said, with a broad, goofy grin.

"If that's the way you fight, then we see eye-to-eye."

The Brantford Bomber winked at McCluskey. *"He's about as wacky as I am,"* McCluskey thought to himself.

Later, back at their rooming house early in the evening of the fight of his life, Gary Broughton and the Brickers slowly prepared to head to the Halifax Forum. As they walked down the driveway towards their car, the boxer turned to the widow who was walking a few steps behind.

"Come along darlin'," he grinned, extending his hand. "Come watch me win."

On Thursday, August 13, 1970, 4,000 spectators entered the Halifax Forum seeking harmless escapist entertainment. They chose the wrong night and the wrong place.

On that evening the aged building on Windsor Street harboured a toxic amalgam of booze, suspicion and racial tension that by night's end would embarrass and frighten the city and further damage a sport already in decline.

Things began well enough, especially for a Rocco Jones promotion. The first two bouts were well-contested and exciting and drew standing ovations.

Then, the main event.

Around 10 pm Gary Broughton entered the ring clad in a fraying robe, rolled-up army socks and antediluvian footwear. Frank Bricker and Tom McCluskey were at his side. Applause equalled jeers as the challenger bumped randomly about the ring awaiting his opponent. A minute later the middleweight champion of Canada advanced along the concrete entranceway, through thick cigarette smoke that had accumulated during the earlier bouts and by now reached the ceiling. With him were Murray Langford, Vince Hennebury, brothers Billy and Donnie, and three or four others

The Broughton strategy: relentlessly attack Downey's body.

pulled aboard by the undertow of drama. Cheers merged with boos and catcalls — the reception now familiar to Downey.

Whatever the greeting, he at least *looked* right. Muttonchop sideburns. Tidy, thick moustache. Hair poised to become a full-blown Afro. A modern warrior and a man of his time, clothed in the lucky red ensemble he had worn for seven years. He skipped up the steps, sprang through the robes and, once inside the ring, performed a set of perfect mid-air splits, legs splayed, arms extended, touching the tips of his boots, as if he were on the dance floor of the Arrows — Sugar Ray Nureyev. His supporters roared.

Broughton says he didn't notice.

Through the opening rounds the challenger displayed a crisp left hand, a weapon that Downey, up on his toes, countered with precise shots and rapid combinations. After five rounds Broughton trailed. However, in the sixth Downey came down off his toes and the Brantford Bomber began to take control, slowing his opponent with body shots — an essential element of his corner's strategy. Downey then elected to alter his tactic and exchange power punches. Seeing this, Broughton's corner encouraged him to press forward even more aggressively and he thumped with right hand after right hand. In the seventh round he hurt Downey twice.

"That tough sonofabitch went out when the bell rang and he fought like you never saw anybody fight before in your life," says

Tom McCluskey. "[He was] just taking him apart and putting him together again."

Between rounds, as Broughton rested on his stool, McCluskey crouched a few inches from his face. "Stay on his body! Forget his head! Beat his body until his arms can't stand up, 'til his legs get rubbery! Don't take no for an answer!"

Sonny MacPhee recalls Downey was comfortably ahead, but in the middle rounds "went back to the corner and the switch turned off. He got up and went out and didn't fight at all. I think Dave fought until there wasn't a tick. There was no way to hold his hands up."

Broughton continued his attack into the eighth when he floored Downey with a left uppercut. "I think I just relaxed for a minute," says Downey. "I went flat-footed for some reason and I was trying to get a shot off and he caught me. I will never forget that punch. And he hit me there — boom! — and I got up too fast. If I'd have stayed down and taken a seven or eight count ... [but] I got up inside of two."

Broughton backpedalled to a neutral corner. As Downey rose to his feet, referee Herb McMullan, his back to Broughton, reached down and began wiping his gloves — a standard duty for referees following a knockdown.

Then came *the incident.*

It began when Broughton suddenly left a neutral corner and darted towards Downey. Accounts of the next few seconds vary significantly.

The *Brantford Expositor* saw Broughton "*colliding* with both the referee and Downey." The Halifax *Chronicle-Herald* said he "brushed past McMullan and *punched* Downey who still had his hands down."

Says Downey, "I was still dazed and I was shaking myself and trying to clear my head, shakin' everything off." He recalls nodding his head to tell his corner he was OK. "Tommy McCluskey was in the [Broughton] corner. Tommy told him you'd better get [him] now and he pushed Broughton out. I didn't see him because [the referee] was in front of me and I'm in my neutral corner and he's got both my hands."

He next remembers Broughton standing over the top of him, throwing "three or four power punches" that landed on the side of his head, near his temple. "That's when the crowd roared."

Broughton recalled things differently.

"Downey got to his feet and the referee started cleaning his gloves," he told the *Expositor*. "He seemed to be taking too long. I moved in and started swinging. One of the punches caught the referee in the nose. This was a championship fight. I wasn't going to give Downey a chance to recover. I've seen it happen too often. If the referee takes too much time, a dazed fighter can come around."

As Broughton completed the assault, scores of Downey's supporters charged from their seats towards the ring. At least one broke through security. Broughton noticed him trying to get through the ropes. He appeared to be brandishing a whisky bottle. "What a hell of a thing!" Broughton told his journalist pal Tom Conway. "I had to keep one eye on Downey and another on this guy. Someone finally pulled him back."

Meanwhile, McMullan tried to reclaim control. He pivoted and warned Broughton, but then astounded everyone when he waved the fighters together, signalling the bout to continue. Broughton immediately lunged at Downey. Still groggy and squeezed into the corner, Downey began to battle back. Punch-for-punch. He maintains today the fight — even at that point — was still his to win, had he not "lost my head." Downey forced Broughton into a corner and pummelled him until the bell rang and then some. "He was goin' down and I was beatin' him on the top of his head."

At the bell McMullan stepped between the fighters and shoved them to their corners.

A minute into the next round, the ninth, Broughton connected with a right, which he later boasted "buried about six inches" into Downey's gut. He followed with a right uppercut flush on Downey's chin. The champion toppled. At 1:47 he was counted out. Newspapers reported he was unconscious for at least three minutes.

"After Downey went down," Broughton recounted to the press, "Frank motioned to me to go after his midsection when he got up.

I looked down and then looked up at Frank and smiled. Downey was stiffer than a board."

Downey disputes the fact the fight ended with him prone. He says he was getting up to go back at Broughton when one of his brothers threw in a towel.

The next day Ace Foley reported that "some of the 4,000 fans wept as their hero took the count."

Many did more than weep.

Before the count-out ended, swarms of patrons rushed the ring. Many made it as far as the apron and were repelled by the boots and fists of McCluskey, Bricker and a few cops who had seen it all coming. Bottles and other objects arched over the heads of the fighters and their handlers, shattering on the wooden chairs and the cement floor below.

Up in the seats there was mayhem. Spectators began exchanging invective, then haymakers. Whites battled blacks, and even women joined the fray. "Everybody started punching everybody else out in the audience," shudders Broughton. "To the left of me and to the right of me, everybody was punching everybody in the face."

Broughton left the ring under police escort, scrambling to cover the 200 or so steps beneath the stands to the dressing rooms, unsure if the mob was headed his way. "In that type of explosion, how can anybody know?"

Along the way Frank Bricker spotted his wife hurrying toward him.

"Get outta here, May!" he shouted, frantically waving her back. "Go get in the car."

Terrified, May Bricker turned around and pushed through the crowd until she reached the Forum parking lot, where she jumped into her Ford sedan and locked all the doors. The friendly widow whom Broughton escorted to the match had already scampered from the Forum "scared stiff," May Bricker recalls.

Meanwhile, Downey made his way back to his dressing room. His memory and reflections of what essentially was a race riot reveals just how far he stood from the racial friction of the time. Somehow, in the middle of it all, an unintentional central figure, he held his emotional distance. "I didn't know who [all these people] were. I didn't know them, so it had no bearings on me."

Extra police were dispatched.

Security guards stood outside Broughton's dressing room, closely watching belligerents roll forward in clusters and then recede. "The heat's on," muttered one guard to another.

Inside a dressing room that had become a bunker, the new middleweight champion of Canada showered and said little. Frank Bricker looked blankly at Tom McCluskey and his brother Ace as thuds echoed on the room's metal door.

"Me just being in Broughton's corner to start with didn't go over very well with all the people backin' Downey," says McCluskey. "He has his followers — nothin' wrong with that. Then to see me in Broughton's corner with Broughton winnin' — that made it all the worse. It took very little to trigger it off. "

As battles raged, a security guard pushed open the door and informed McCluskey that some guy had just struck his other brother Cobey, who had been talking with a couple of Nova Scotia Voyageurs down the hallway. Seeing the bedlam and probably fearing they would be next, the hockey players had taken off. Tom and Ace charged out of the dressing room and whacked the three assailants, who then immediately fled down past the Forum canteen and kept on going.

When the McCluskeys returned to the dressing room "all hell broke out. They just pushed the cops all over the place and a bunch of white guys got beat up in the parking lot. So they were pounding on the dressing room door tryin' to get into the dressing room. And Broughton got scared shitless. There had to be 300 people — easy — in the lobby."

Broughton looked at Tom McCluskey. "They won't do nothin' to me, will they?"

"I don't know," said McCluskey, "but I think I know who they want."

Broughton does not recall being especially frightened. "I knew the door was locked and there were four of us. And how many can come in through the door at any one time? I can fight. I wasn't nervous, but I was excited because I won the fight."

After an hour a cop rapped at the door and discreetly escorted Broughton and Bricker to the Forum box office. The peaceful journey terminated with Rocco Jones handing the fighter a cheque for $1,000. The Brantford Bomber grinned.

Meanwhile, alone in her sedan in a parking lot in the middle of a war zone hundreds of miles from home, May Bricker whispered a prayer and waited. "I got into the car and started the engine. I said to myself that Frank and Gary will probably make a dash across the parking lot and I'll have the engine running. Which is what I did. Every policeman in Halifax was there. I'm just scared to death. The cops brought them out — Gary and Frank. They were shakin', too. They were just upset to no end. I opened the door and said, 'Get in!' "

They sped away at 1 am.

In his dressing room David Downey seethed as Vince Hennebury proclaimed that — any second now! — he was about to march down the hall and kick the royal shit out of the guys in Broughton's corner. He overcame the urge.

At the peak of the trouble police asked Downey to come out and try to calm his fans. He initially refused but eventually emerged and assured those who remained that *he* had won. That Broughton should have been disqualified. That at the very least the match should have been ruled no contest.

"Him takin' *my* title. Hey, if *I* did that ...."

According to Downey, at some point during the commotion Broughton had stood in the doorway of his dressing room and said he was sorry.

"David, you got the next fight," Broughton promised. But the rematch wouldn't happen immediately. Five weeks later Broughton fought Joe Blair in Windsor, Ontario, for $200, in a match that likely had been arranged for some time.

In addition, Broughton apologized in the press — to both Downey and referee Herb McMullan — for his actions in the eighth round. "I was just over-anxious. I just couldn't wait. I could see the championship. I wish I hadn't done it."

The events of that night would linger a few more weeks for Tom, Ace and Cobey McCluskey. The three local men whom Tom had assailed as he came to Cobey's aid near Broughton's dressing room had pressed assault charges. Partly galled and partly amused, the McCluskeys retained a lawyer. One morning they all headed for the courthouse.

In the lobby Tom noticed three uneasy fellows outside the courtroom. He thought, "*Those gotta be the three guys. They don't know one McCluskey from another, eh? They don't know who hit who. They haven't got a clue.*"

Tom approached the trio.

"Howya doin', guys?"

"Who're you?"

"I'm Tom McCluskey."

"You broke my teeth!" said one.

"You broke my nose!" said another.

"Wasn't me," said McCluskey. "Naw, not *me*. Wasn't me." After a few seconds of silence, he continued. "You guys ever been in a fight before, or is this the first time?"

"We been in fights," came a piqued reply from one of the men.

"Well, is this what happened every time somebody hit you guys? Did you take them to court? Jesus, I wish I had a dollar for every time somebody hit me. If *I* took *them* to court, we'd be here for a lifetime."

McCluskey slowly shook his head. "I really don't understand you guys. I thought you were tougher than that."

With this, one accuser turned to another and shouted, "I *told* you! You shouldn't be takin' this man to court! What they gonna say about it? I don't want it! I'm no baby! I don't want nothin' to do with this!"

McCluskey nodded. "Then what ya doin' here?"

"Somebody said come to court, so we came to court."

McCluskey gestured for his lawyer and, in front of the three men, informed him, "*Those* guys don't want to take us to court. Somebody talked them into this crap."

A short time later all six men walked away.

9

REVIVED

The 18 weeks between the madness of the first Broughton fight and the rematch were excruciating for Downey, without his title, politely parrying those who innocently rubbed salt in the wound.

In his three years as champion he had revelled in the noble standing the title conferred, if only to North Enders. And now he was left to explain over and over that he was caught off guard, that it was a dirty punch, that the ref was in the way, that Broughton should have been disqualified, that it should have been declared no contest.

"When he walked into the room, all you'd have to say is 'Here's the champ' or 'Hi champ,'" says Harris Sullivan. "He'd be like a little kid, like he was 10 years old. He loved the idea of being champion. He liked the perks. He liked the attention. Simple. Most people do, anyway, but he *particularly* did."

Broadcaster Alex J. Walling first met Downey at the Halifax Forum in a tiny room used for press conferences. "I'm waiting there and I think he's deliberately 10 minutes late. And all of a sudden this stream of people comes in. You'd think it was Ali. I could tell which one was Dave. Oh m' God, yes. All dolled-up! Looked great." Walling still remembers the boxer wore a gold and white polyester outfit, with a black shirt and gold tie "straight out of Studio 54."

While Downey stewed in Halifax, 1000 miles to the west the new champion was enjoying his new status.

"Y'know," Gary Broughton reflected in a Kitchener pub between swallows, "for the rest of my life, they'll never be able to take away from me that I was the middleweight champion of Canada."

Broughton and Frank Bricker set up camp in Detroit to prepare for the December rematch. However, a torn muscle in his right forearm confined his training mainly to roadwork until about three weeks before the rematch. A significant difference in the second fight would be that Bricker would command Broughton's corner without Tom McCluskey, the chief strategist in his win four months earlier.

Meanwhile, Downey trained in New York City, compliments of Victor Beed. At Goldman's Gym he took instruction from the aptly named Harry Wiley, a 63-year-old sage renowned for his success with Sugar Ray Robinson. Unlike other celebrated and handsomely compensated trainers who would deign little attention to transients, Wiley was attentive. "He made me feel good in that fight," states Downey.

Wiley took his Nova Scotian pupil to various gyms around the city, including the famous Gleason's, exposing him to several top fighters in his weight class. "Everybody's gym was different. Every gym had a lot of rough guys there."

In one of these establishments during a workout Downey first met Sugar Ray Robinson. The encounter did not go well.

Robinson's trainer, George Gainford, who knew Downey from an earlier trip to the United States, offered to make the introduction and walked with Downey in Robinson's direction. Gainford backed off when he noticed the legend was taping his hands to work out. "He don't like to be bothered," the trainer whispered. They tried again, a few minutes later.

"This is the Canadian fighter I was talkin' about," Gainford said. Robinson extended his hand. "That was like gold," Downey recalls.

Later that day Robinson asked for someone to spar with a Puerto Rican kid he was tutoring. Gainford volunteered Downey. In the ring the kid immediately went on the attack, violating the usual protocol for such exercises and surprising Downey who for protection tucked his head between his gloves, turtle fashion. Not only was Downey getting slapped around, it was happening right in front of his hero. It would not continue.

In the next round the Halifax fighter retaliated, opening up on his opponent, knocking him across the ring, buckling his knees. Robinson screamed at the kid in Spanish. Gainford yelled for Downey to ease up. His commands were ignored. After another round Downey left the ring and approached Robinson, hoping for a few pointers and, maybe, a little praise.

"When I came out and went to ask him something, he walked right away from me. Just turned his back. I was stunned. I was disappointed because this is the man I idolized."

Robinson refused to speak to him the rest of the afternoon.

Nevertheless, Downey's overall preparation under Harry Wiley was going well. Wiley regularly informed the Halifax media that Downey was focused, co-operative and primed. Not only was he an unofficial press agent, apparently Wiley was also a sorcerer. Early in the camp he introduced into Downey's diet a 'secret remedy' that included raw meat along with marinated eggs, beaten but not cooked. Wiley promised the fighter it would turn him into a savage animal. The boxer nearly vomited just looking at it.

"Harry, I don't want to be like no animal," Downey would protest — before closing his eyes and consuming the concoction.

New York also provided Downey with his most treasured personal encounter. The men working with him were at the same time helping Muhammad Ali prepare for his bout with a burly Argentine named Oscar Bonavena.

On the evening of Ali's match, one of his aides escorted Downey to the lobby of Manhattan's Waldorf Astoria. There he watched in wonder as the heavyweight legend strutted for television cameras, engulfed by sycophants and admirers, including wealthy businessmen and Hollywood stars. Downey especially noted a black leather coat Ali was wearing. "I had a leather coat that was long," remembers Downey, "but mine wasn't like his because his was a *real* expensive one. Fur all along the neck and down the sides."

A few moments passed as Downey stood amid the commotion that for Ali had become a way of life. Eventually Harry Wiley and Jimmy Ellis, a sparring partner of Ali's and himself a future heavyweight champion, walked over. Downey had met Ellis in the gym a few days before, and now the friendly Kentuckian began encouraging him to — Jesus! — *approach Ali*. Downey meekly moved across the lobby a half-step behind Wiley and Ellis. "This is the fighter I told you about, from Canada," Wiley informed Ali when they reached the great man's side.

Ali smiled slightly, then reached down and clasped Downey's hand. The two men locked eyes for a second or two before Ali turned away to continue flirting with an impeccably coiffured middle-aged blond woman that Downey later realized was movie star Lana Turner. "Lana Turner! It blew my mind as soon as they said that!" Still, he felt snubbed, but only a little. He understood the moment and understood the demands. Recalling his disheartening encounter with Sugar Ray Robinson he gently withdrew.

As he began his retreat Downey heard someone shout after him.

"Hey! Hey! Where you goin'?"

He looked back over his shoulder. It was one of Ali's bodyguards. "Muhammad wants you to come back. You're walkin' away from him."

"He's talking, and I ain't gonna interfere. I got introduced, so I'll just go over there and …"

As he spoke, Downey noticed Ali striding toward him.

"Where you goin'?' " Ali demanded.

"I didn't wanna rain on your talkin'," Downey smiled and — incredibly — once more began to walk away. On about the fourth stride he felt a firm hand on his shoulder. It squeezed hard and yanked him around.

Ali again, and he wanted to play.

"He starts jabbin' and stickin' his hands out. I start jabbin' and throwin' back and I'm throwin' my hands quick. The guy told him how quick I could jab. My hands were just as quick as his. I'm throwin' mine and he was throwin' his and I could feel the wind comin' — boom-boom-boom-boom-boom-boom — and I could feel the wind because they were missing me by about six inches. He's six-foot-four or so. After that was done I said to someone that I thought he was gonna hit me in the nose. When he was doing it, his hand was stretched out as long as it could go and I was wondering how it was he was just missing me.

"I thought to myself, '*What if this man had smacked me in my nose or somethin*'? What would I do, right in the Waldorf in front of all them people?' I'd probably have tried to take a shot back at him! Then, if I actually struck him, and something happened, and he couldn't fight ... all the money!"

Following the amusing barrage 'The Greatest' wrapped his arms around the only middleweight from North End Halifax he ever knew. "See ya at the fight," Ali said.

Minutes later Downey found himself in the hotel dining room with Ali's parents, Cassius and Odessa Clay. Cassius immediately ordered him a steak. "I sat there with them. Well, I didn't *want* to eat. I didn't want nothin' but they all ordered steak and everything and I had to eat it. They ordered *me* a steak!"

At some point in the evening Ali's brother Rudy passed Downey a ticket to see Ali–Bonavena live at Madison Square Garden. Downey didn't go. Feeling that it would take hours to get from the Garden to his room in the Bronx, he instead went with a friend to a 125th Street movie theatre showing the fight on closed circuit television. He retained the Garden ticket as a souvenir.

In December 1970, Gary Broughton returned to Nova Scotia, the land of his conquest, employing the argot of a puncher and delighting a handful of reporters content to fill their notebooks with nonsense.

"I noted in the paper that Downey has a secret remedy to make him strong," the Brantford Bomber sneered. "Well, I just like to say that I've been drinking a lot of tea and I feel fit and strong."

While Broughton indulged the Halifax media, Downey and Wiley struggled just to get into town. A snowstorm in New York grounded some flights and delayed others. Finally landing in Montreal, they spent the night before the fight at Laval Airport with Downey trying — unsuccessfully — to sleep on an airport bench. They arrived in Halifax on the evening of the fight, racing the 40 miles from the airport to the Forum, screeching up to the entrance as the semi-final bout began. Downey sprinted to his dressing room, leapt on a set of scales and donned his new colours: black and gold. A half-hour later — "I didn't get a chance to get a sweat on me" — he stood at ring centre eyeing the Brantford Bomber.

In the first three rounds Downey glided, showing no signs of his strenuous journey. His head bobbed and ducked as he dodged Broughton's looping rights and turned the champion's normally efficient, piston-like jabs into clumsy lunges. Downey moved constantly and pressed his own jabs into Broughton's reddening face.

"Stand still!" barked Broughton as the pair waltzed at ring centre.

"*I* don't have to stand still!" replied Downey, snapping off two more jabs.

But Downey's dominance ebbed. In the fourth, Broughton scored early with a right cross that chastised his challenger. Downey responded with a flashing combination that pushed Broughton to the ropes. For the rest of the fight they would exchange solid blows, neither man going down. In the sixth, Broughton opened a cut over Downey's left eye. But his corner closed the wound and Downey adroitly protected it for the remainder of the contest.

On the strength of his early dominance, Downey was awarded a split decision. Quipped Broughton, "I wish I had a vote."

This time at the announcement the spectators stayed in their seats.

"He was always out of my reach," offered Broughton, resigned to his fate. "When you've lost 19 fights as I have, you learn to roll with the losses."

"I'd love to give him another fight," smiled Downey.

Broughton's manager Frank Bricker called it a hometown decision delivered only because Downey did not get knocked out. "How can you win a fight running?" Bricker bitched.

Ace Foley shared Bricker's assessment and urged another match. "While a patient Johan Louw of Edmonton deserves the next shot at the title, a third meeting between Downey and Broughton is still very much in the minds of rabid local fight fans. They make merry music together."

For a while it looked as though Johan Louw would finally get a shot at the title.

The first man Louw ever opposed in a boxing ring he flattened with a head butt. "The blacks on the [South African] farm used to fight by head-butting and it was the only way I knew." Louw soon learned other ways and in the mid-1960s won a South African amateur championship. He later turned pro to help finance his schooling, which in 1968 brought him to the University of Alberta in pursuit of a master's degree in physical education.

Louw primed for fights with manic fervour — hours in the gym, miles of roadwork. By fight time his ill-temper scared even his own handlers. Once he tried to kick an opponent's trainer after (mistakenly) thinking the trainer had showered him with liquid during the fight. Louw later apologized for the attack. He made no apology for his intensity.

By 1971, however, his allegiance to the sport was flagging. Although he had been the top Canadian middleweight contender for more than a year — amassing a record of 14-1 and earning the epithet 'Fighting Scholar' — he had grown frustrated over his inability to get Downey into the ring. A deal the year before had fallen through, but the autumn of 1971 furnished another chance. Downey's team had tentatively agreed to a title match in November or December.

First, however, Louw signed on as part of a double main event at Dartmouth Memorial Arena in October. It was the first professional card sanctioned by the new Dartmouth Boxing Commission, formed to bring control and credibility to the sport in that city. It brought neither.

Trouble began when Louw's opponent, Don Turner, refused to come to Halifax, believing that promoter Rocco Jones was going to stiff him for the flight home to New York. A replacement fighter from Virginia never made it to town either, after an airline misplaced his ticket.

On learning all this, Downey pulled out of his bout with Thurman 'Doc' Holliday, a 24-year-old former U.S. Marine. He reasoned he should not give Louw a chance to observe him up close when he couldn't do the same. When people telephoned Downey beseeching him to reconsider, he hung up. A city alderman also failed to get him to reconsider. So did his brother Billy, a co-promoter who would lose $4,000 on the venture.

"A fiasco," observed the Fighting Scholar to a local sportswriter, "is a very mild description of this situation."

The card was cancelled.

Holliday's manager Chris Cline vowed to campaign for Downey's suspension and bring the matter before World Boxing Association president Bill Brennan, his "close personal friend." CPBF vice-president Gerry Spears considered suspending all parties. Only the *Chronicle-Herald's* Ken Jennex sympathized — with Rocco Jones, at least. "When a boxing card is called off the first person to be criticized is the promoter. LeRoy Rocco Jones quite often has received adverse publicity in his past promotions. However, the circumstances leading up to the cancellation of Saturday night's card in Dartmouth cannot be blamed on Jones as he did everything in his power to put the fight on."

The episode was most unfortunate for Johan Louw, out of pocket and soon out of boxing, his best chance at a national championship forsaken amid blunder and intransigence that Nova Scotia autumn.

For Downey, the Louw incident blended into a lengthy, damaging lull that stretched from December 1970, after he recovered the middleweight championship from Gary Broughton, to June 1972, when he faced an American in a non-title bout. Downey continued to train, but few outside his immediate circle noticed.

The reason for this withdrawal, he explains, was simple: the right offer never materialized. The one accompanied by a purse of championship stature, with an opponent worthy of the occasion. "They weren't going to throw me to the wolves," he says.

Still, this 18-month absence could not have been more ill-timed. Not only did it occur in his prime years, the late 20s — the fleeting apogee in a prizefighter's career when the mental and the physical intersect — but it also coincided with the awakening of his city, revitalizing its facade and its soul.

Halifax was on the move — in all directions, but mostly up.

"The new Halifax is big enough to be important [and the] environment is magnificent," *Maclean's* announced in January 1970 in a seven-page homage to all things cosmopolitan.

Proof of the magnificence abounded.

A 21-storey downtown apartment building called One Sackville Place altered the city's skyline and introduced to Halifax a *nouveau* lifestyle appealing to young professionals. The $3.5-million, 13-storey Royal Bank Building, the 10-storey Halifax Insurance Building and the 10-storey Hollis Building were among several new downtown office towers entrenching Halifax as Atlantic Canada's financial and commercial centre.

The city's brightest emblem of urban transformation was Scotia Square, a $54-million alloy of apartments, office space and upscale boutiques that granted Halifax big-city *cachet.* Scotia Square opened in late 1970, the culmination of intricate financing and dealmaking by a swashbuckling developer named Charles MacCulloch, a rags-to-riches local boy who resembled Howard Hughes in appearance and — to some extent — deed. The project included 11 new buildings and 19 acres of redeveloped land, making it the largest concrete commercial structure in the country, grander than Montreal's sexy Place Ville Marie.

Diesel buses replaced electric trolleys and brought big-city air pollution to street level. New roads enhanced travel around the area, with the greatest improvement resulting from the completion of the A. Murray MacKay Bridge, an eight-tenths of a mile suspension bridge spanning the site of the infamous Halifax Explosion.

For eight frantic days in August 1969 Halifax and Dartmouth hosted the first Canada Summer Games. The games drew several hundred amateur athletes, and left behind a massive recreational infrastructure that included a 10,000-seat stadium, an eight-lane track, six tennis courts and improvements to innumerable existing facilities, including the Bedford Basin Yacht Club and the Halifax Forum. The event marshalled more than 2,000 volunteers and immense civic pride, all for $1.8 million, most of it from Ottawa.

High-rise buildings and high-profile games melded with even more fundamental shifts.

The long-entrenched religious divide between Catholics and Protestants narrowed considerably. The waterfront was transformed by Canada's first terminal built to handle container shipping.

Nevertheless, shipping and manufacturing were challenged by education and health as pillars of the area's economy. Jobs increased for teachers, lawyers, architects, businessmen, doctors and other medical professionals. The city's two main universities — Dalhousie and St. Mary's — both lavished millions on new facilities, highlighted by Dal's new $16-million life sciences centre.

The city also grew physically. In 1969 it amalgamated five suburbs, quadrupling its area and boosting its population to 225,000, surpassing cities such as Victoria and Regina. Demographics were also altered by newcomers and by local young people choosing to forgo the habitual exodus to bigger cities such as Toronto and Boston.

"People wanted to make things happen," says Walter Fitzgerald, North End alderman during the period. "People wanted to make things work. You'd have a meeting and jeez the place'd be packed — with black and white and everybody'd be talking and arguing and at the end of the night everybody'd get together, [at least] enough to move forward."

In the age of protest, Halifax shouted with discontent. Haligonians marched as part of the International Day of Protest against the Vietnam War and decried the U.S. detonation of a 1.2-megaton thermonuclear device off Alaska. Hippies camped out in a small park across from the Nova Scotian Hotel, and 30 'long-hairs' staged a sit-in at a Spring Garden Road restaurant that refused them service. Halifax even hosted a two-day seminar starring the man the *4th Estate* billed 'the most feared social activist in modern time,' Saul Alinsky.

Sports also electrified the city, led by St. Mary's University's flourishing athletic program, which garnered national hockey, basketball and football championships win. "There's a danger of being known as a jock school," athletic director Bob Hayes acknowledged. "But not being known as anything is the alternative that I see."

The Nova Scotia Voyageurs hockey club made history in 1972

when, in its inaugural season, it became the first Canadian team ever to win the American Hockey League championship. It was coached by Cape Breton-born Al MacNeil.

Halifax's cultural scene matured, led by its entertainment sector that seemed to brighten overnight. Gerald Regan recalls that in the 1950s and early 1960s a restaurant called Lohnes' on downtown Blowers Street was "the principal upper-class restaurant. [It] used to close at six o'clock at night. Why would anyone be downtown in the evening?"

New liquor laws and regulations for bars and restaurants swept aside Victorian notions of female fragility and finally permitted men and women to drink spirits together in public. A more vivacious — and more racially diverse — bar and club scene emerged. The Misty Moon Show Bar booked the region's top rock bands. The New Zodiac presented acts such as Michael Safi and his Harem Revue. The Herring Choker attracted the likes of Saul's Good Time Jug Band. And the Lobster Trap tendered employment to 'classy' skimpily clad *artistes* bearing monikers such as Bambi and Amber.

A conspicuous black night-spot of the era was The Club Unusual. Located in the North End, its house band included 19-year-old singer Linda Gordon, who claimed membership in the black power–influenced Afro-Canadian Liberation Movement, and 30-year-old pianist Joe Sealy, who would mature into one of the city's most popular entertainers. "Halifax in 1955 was worse than the Deep South," Sealy told *Maclean's* in the late 1960s. "There was no formal colour bar. Just unwritten rules. [Now] the ghetto mentality is going. Black people are beginning to go out — being part of the community."

While other clubs made their mark, none demonstrated the city's transformation as robustly as the Arrows Club, which hosted Stokely Carmichael for one memorable evening during the Black Panther's visit to Halifax in 1968.

A weathered soul brother named Little Royal brays familiar lyrics in front of a six-piece band as the whole place writhes, and each note pulsates through the limbs.

"I'm gonna take you high-uh ... baby, baby, baby, baby ... high-uh ... gonna take you high-uh ...

Little Royal, glistening sweat, leaps from the stage, slides to a nearby table and thrusts a microphone into the face of a young white woman and screams, *"High-uh."*

And the young white woman whispers, *"High-uh."*

"High-uh!" he demands.

"High-uh," she sings.

"High-uh!" he screams.

"High-uh," she sings louder, finally.

And then Little Royal slides to another table and thrusts the microphone into the face of the premier of the province of New Brunswick and screams *"High-uh!"*

And the gadfly politician grins and fires back, *"High-uh!"*

"High-uh!" sings Little Royal.

"High-uh!" shouts Richard Hatfield.

And then Little Royal slides to another table and jabs the microphone into the face of the middleweight champion of the nation and screams, *"High-uh!"*

And the boxer springs from his seat and leans into the mike and shrieks, *"High-uh!"*

"High-uh!" sings Little Royal.

"High-uh!" sings David Downey.

Welcome to the Arrows Club, Soul Centre of the Maritimes, circa 1971. On Brunswick Street, in the shadow of the Old Town Clock. Two dollars cover charge. Open until 3:30 am. Cheapest beer in town.

Out of sight! Blow your mind! Do your thing!

And somewhere in the crowd, writer Silver Donald Cameron is taking notes while David's older brother, Billy, slaps his hands in rhythm and visualizes his bank balance climbing *high-uh*.

"It would be silly to regard Downey and the Arrows as the cultural voice of the black revolution in Halifax," wrote Cameron in the *Scotian Journalist.* "[Billy] Downey is no radical, no prophet, no organizer. He had a good idea, worked diligently to see it realized — and he struck the public fancy.

"But [neither should the Arrows] be taken for less than it is: a

Billy Downey (left) with Gerald Regan at the Arrows Club.

thoroughly enjoyable place which is probably the best entertainment value in the Maritimes. A place where the white Maritimer can at least sample some of the riches of the black culture. A place where he can think again, perhaps, about the fact that half the black people in Canada live along the back roads and in the poorer urban quarters of Nova Scotia."

"I was the big black man in the city at that time," smiles Billy today.

"I went there many times," says Gerald Regan, who as a provincial MLA represented the North End, and who brought along chums and associates to build up contacts between the communities. "I thought that they and their friends were reflective of the black community — and very strongly supported by the black community — not people who had more aggressive or Black Panther sort of leanings."

The Arrows happened in stages. First as a hole-in-the-wall North End disco on Creighton Street in the early '60s, then for eight years around the corner on Agricola and finally, in 1970, downtown into what had been an old empty garage. After $20,000 in renovations the Downeys were proprietors of Halifax's festal premises of the era. The *in* spot in town. "Big dance floor, big stage, very garish," recalls Harris Sullivan.

Big nights saw 500 people file down a small, dark hallway lined with framed photos of the acts and the owners. Although the Downeys certainly did not deliberately *intend* the club as a racial confluence, whites comprised 85 percent of the customers on weekdays and 50 per cent on weekends.

Most acts were American, high-octane blues and funk, just a hit single away from continental renown. They cost the Downeys about $2,000 a week, but gave three or four shows a night and held nothing back. Dynamic Superiors Review. The Fabulous Sundia and Full Speed. Soul Brothers Six. Flame N' King and His Bold Ones. Ben E. King. Tobias. Sam and Dave. The Blue Notes. Teddy Pendergrass. Jackson Brown.

Billy got Ike and Tina Turner "dirt cheap" just before they emerged as one of the foremost acts of the era. He says he and the duo would kill an afternoon in Montreal's Esquire Showbar when his schedule as a train porter would take him to that city. He recalls Ike "hitting her in the ass with the guitar" and having her shimmy just for the hell of it.

For Billy Downey, the Arrows' success came fast and at a price. "The club was like a play-toy to me. It messed up my married life and I used it bad. That's what most club owners do. I had the world at my feet. Anything I touched used to turn to gold at that time."

Arrows' patrons included businessmen, judges, entertainers — Anne Murray gave an impromptu performance — and media types.

Many politicians also took in the ambience. Gerald Regan remembers escorting fellow premiers there. One unexpected guest was laconic federal opposition leader Robert Stanfield, who dropped in one evening to check out the place where his daughter was spending so much time. "I guess the kids like it," he conceded to Billy over some high-volume music.

Sports personalities included broadcaster Danny Gallivan, hockey standout Bobby Hull, baseball stars Maury Wills and Ferguson Jenkins, and football all-star Billy 'White Shoes' Johnson. Heavyweight champion Joe Frazier and his trainer Yancy Durham

Billy Downey (right) with Montreal Canadiens coach Claude Ruel, an Arrows Club regular.

became friends of Billy's, as did former Montreal Canadiens coach Claude Ruel. Many Nova Scotia Voyageurs were regulars.

There was the odd confrontation, of course. CFL lineman Angelo Mosca was a problem once or twice, and Pittsburgh Steeler running back Franco Harris "went crazy" when Billy insisted he follow club rules and check his hat at the door. Harris eventually relented. One crowded night a well-known national television newsman loudly shared his views about "niggers." Graham Downey intercepted Billy and a group of Americans intent on heaving him out onto the sidewalk.

"The Arrows Club seemed to defuse some racial tension in the city, thanks to the Downeys," says Pat Connolly. "It was the way they ran it. It was the way that they treated people. It was the way they melded the solitudes and said this is not a black club *per se*, and it's open to everybody — white clients, black clients, red clients, whatever."

Yet amid relentless change in the city and harmony in the Arrows Club, the issue of race remained. Incidents continued along a brittle fault line, including an episode that centred on a 19-year-old black high school student named Ronnie Drummond.

Late one night in March 1970 Drummond was standing on Creighton Street when police arrived and accused of him of loitering. One officer cuffed his hands behind his back, threw him in the back seat of the cruiser and pummelled him with his right fist. At the police station the handcuffs were removed but the cop continued to beat him until other officers intervened. "I was bleeding in the police station and this guy still kept trying to hit me," Drummond, who was charged with resisting arrest, told the *4th Estate*. "You're damn right I resisted. I knew what they were going to do."

When activist Buddy Daye arrived at the police station the next morning to assist Drummond, he found bruises on the teenager's head and bloody wounds near his mouth. "It shakes my faith in something I believed in," he said. "The kid had been beaten, he was scared and they wouldn't even let him make one phone call."

A week after the incident Mayor Allan O'Brien conceded that city police required special training. "I think it's sort of commonplace in the white community in Nova Scotia to have some prejudices whether we are aware of them or not, and policemen are recruited into the force with all the natural bias of the community as a whole."

10

CANDY-MAN

While Halifax sailed into a new age, the local daily press remained anchored in the 1940s. Indeed, the Halifax Herald Ltd. — publisher of the morning *Chronicle-Herald* and the afternoon *Mail-Star* — appeared oblivious to the powerful currents of the century's most raucous period.

While the papers managed to attract some skilled journalists and remained profitable for their owners, the Dennis family, they were frequently timid and often embarrassing. Political reportage was superficial, sports coverage was shallow and major issues such as local race relations were never broached in any significant way. In 1970 the Davey Senate Committee on Mass Media concluded that no Canadian city was as badly served by its daily newspapers.

It was not always so.

Both papers could trace their origin to Joseph Howe, one of the province's most important and beloved historical figures who, in the first half of the 19th century, led the fight for freedom of the press and free speech. Howe was a great orator and considered one of Canada's finest journalists. He also became premier later in life.

In 1844 he founded the *Novascotian*, and then co-founded the *Morning Chronicle*. A rival paper, the *Morning Herald*, came along in 1875. The *Herald* with its sister afternoon paper the *Mail*, and the *Chronicle* with its afternoon paper the *Star* were each other's main competition for more than half a century. In 1949 both sets of papers had merged to become the *Chronicle-Herald* and *Mail-Star* respectively, under control of the Dennis family. They would have a local daily newspaper monopoly until the arrival of the *Daily News* four decades later.

In the 1960s and 1970s the only other mainstream print entity in the area was the weekly *Dartmouth Free Press*. A volatile left-wing alternative press — which frequently mocked the Halifax Herald Ltd. and dubbed it 'The Old Lady Of Argyle Street' — was led by the *4th Estate* and its offshoot, the *Scotian Journalist*. In 1973 the *Scotian Journalist* won a prestigious Roland Michener Award for Journalism for its investigative report on the poor conditions at a home for women in New Brunswick. "The only professional in the place is myself," gloated publisher and editor Frank Fillmore to the *Globe and Mail*. "We have a young staff who are underpaid, misused and abused, but they have a lot of enthusiasm." The city also had two television stations and a handful of radio stations, most with smallish news departments.

As Halifax became less conservative, its television and radio stations began allocating more resources to diversions such as sports, experimenting with formats and attracting neophytes smitten with aggressive American media techniques. As a result, sports coverage was uneven, occasionally bizarre, but in spots vivacious and gutsy. Ultimately, most of the city's 20 to 30 sports reporters — almost all of them men — were cheerleaders.

But not all.

Newcomers such as Doug Saunders, first of CHNS then of the CBC, began challenging practices and attitudes, as did his pal, 25-year-old Quebec City native Alex J. Walling, who joined CHNS and straightaway invited comparisons to Howard Cosell — a semblance Walling never discouraged.

Other notable personalities in the Halifax market included CFDR's Pat Connolly, whose even-handed style made him the most approachable of the local cast, Gerry Fogarty of CBH radio, an erudite former general reporter of scholarly appearance, and Steve Armitage of CBHT television, the possessor of the corporation look that would eventually procure him a job with *Hockey Night In Canada*.

The transition of the craft in Halifax, however, was epitomized by two men, separated by two generations and disparate philosophies.

Ace Foley was a disciple of the 1920s 'Golden Age of Sport', when in the U.S. high-profile sportswriters presented successful athletes as real-life Horatio Alger characters. For his entire career he practised the Golden Age's charitable posture and journalistic deportment, long after they had become anachronisms as quaint as his ever-present fedora and cigar.

A Halifax native, Foley, who stood less than five feet tall, started writing sports for the Halifax *Chronicle* in 1920, at age 15. For half a century he was sports editor at the *Herald* — a lengthy tenure that locked him into a single, parochial perspective and made him a *de facto* model and mentor to at least three generations of Nova Scotia sportswriters. "Growing up I didn't want to be Rocket Richard or Frank Sobey or Bob Stanfield," said *Chronicle-Herald* sports columnist Hugh Townsend, one such understudy. "I wanted to be Ace Foley."

In the last two decades of his career Foley attended fewer sports events, doing most of his writing from the isolation of his desk at the newspaper's offices downtown. It showed. His column became a mistake-prone, walk-down-memory-lane affirmation of a journalistic dotage at once both sweet and sad.

Foley's antithesis was Harris Sullivan, an audacious young Monctonian whose near-shoulder length hair, drooping moustache and penetrating squint announced his politics and got up the noses of the local reporting establishment. He was not an admirer of Foley's work.

"Harris was unafraid of calling the shots that he felt needed critical attention," says Pat Connolly, who along with others was emboldened by Sullivan's technique of editorializing in his daily coverage.

As a teenager Sullivan worked summers at the Moncton *Times Transcript*. At age 19 he was already a manager of the morning paper. Shortly afterwards he came to Halifax and radio station CJCH. His hours were long, his approach brazen. His 'Goat-of-the-Day' feature, a sharp 30-second tag at the end of his daily radio sportscasts, focused chiefly on poor performances by local athletes. He felt the heat. When Sullivan appeared at centre ice at the

Halifax Forum in between-period promotions during Junior A hockey games, he would be booed more lustily than the visiting team. "There could be 5000 people in the Forum and you couldn't hear anything for a good minute-and-a-half to two minutes because of the constant booing because I was introduced. I remember one day [my girlfriend] was in tears because of this universal hatred that was coming down."

Eventually his interests swung to politics and hard news. In the Halifax of the 1960s and 1970s, this meant race relations. And no reporter in the Maritimes was better equipped or positioned to tackle such a powerful, complex story. His recurrent coverage of Halifax's black-white dilemma was extraordinary, award-winning journalism. Most notable was *Encounter,* a week-long television series that each night laid bare the city's racial problems and civic challenges such as urban development. While the black community received him with some suspicion, Sullivan leveraged his identity as a sportscaster to open doors that had been slammed in the faces of other reporters.

In Downey, Halifax's sports journalists shared a conundrum— a disconnect between prizefighter and press. Several things contributed to the disconnect, but perhaps most stark was a divergent perspective on the importance of the middleweight title.

"He could never even fathom why it didn't mean to others what it meant to him," reflects Doug Saunders. "He thought by being the Canadian middleweight boxing champion that he had somehow bestowed this enormous honour or gift on Nova Scotia or Halifax and he could never ever understand why it was not perceived as such. He believed that he was this wonderful ambassador for Halifax and Nova Scotia.

"He lent a lot more credence to the fact that he was Canadian champion than just about anyone else did. There may have been a time — in fact I know there was because I know about the history of boxing in this province — when it was very significant to be the Canadian middleweight boxing champion. To my way of thinking, by the time Dave was champion it had lost some of its lustre."

"He was the Canadian champion," Alex J. Walling scornfully

points out. "He walked around here as if he were Muhammad Ali. Nice guy, lovable, quotable. But he was not Muhammad Ali. Canadian championship my ass."

"Dave Downey sort of lived under the illusion that because he was Canadian middleweight champion the promoters should be flocking to his door," says Gerry Fogarty, of CBC Radio. "But Dave didn't seem to understand that the Canadian middleweight championship means nothing if you don't have a fighting champion and you don't have good challengers."

Another puzzle for the media was that, as both man and athlete, Downey did not follow usual behaviour patterns.

"He was a very enigmatic character," says Connolly. "[It was] difficult for the media to understand where he was coming from and where he was going because he put the brakes on his career with some frequency. He'd sort of disappear from the scene for a while, then pop back in again. He would go off on these training cruises in New York or Boston or wherever and [then] nothing would ever happen. So that's kind of a confusing situation."

Connolly says the media was not stacked against Downey, as much as he liked to think so. "[The] athlete can only win by performing. But he's not going to win much by regarding the media as the opponent. I don't think that Dave really understood that."

While Downey perplexed the media, the reverse was also true.

He simply could not understand why local reporters would portray him adversely, refusing to assign him the respect owed a Canadian champion and the favour due a tribune of the North End. Instead he felt the media indifferent and sporadically caustic. Downey continually wondered why. Was he not skilled, successful, accommodating, clean-living and quotable? Was there a better role model for North End youth? Were his fights not exciting?

"No matter who I'd fight [it] wasn't enough for here — nobody nowhere else would ever say that. Only here in Halifax. I beat everybody that they brought. So what more do I have to do? That should be enough."

He speculates the press resented that he enjoyed his success so much. "Well, you *have* to enjoy it. If you go out there before four or five or six thousand fans, and you display yourself and do what you want to do after training for months and months, and you've been away from your family and you do something great, you have to go out and be proud of what you did. If you are not proud, then what was the purpose of doing it?"

In June 1972, Downey ended his 18-month absence from the ring with a flourish, fighting twice in the same month. He won both matches.

The first was a dreary 10-round technical knockout of six-foot-one Thurman 'Doc' Holliday, who had left Nova Scotia in a snit eight months before when Downey withdrew from a planned card that also featured Johan Louw. Now Holliday, a native of Ohio, had returned for the 'grudge match' packing the 'Downey Doodle,' a purported paralyzing punch he claimed to have learned from no less a celebrity than convicted murderer Dr. Sam Shepard. He further taunted Downey by boasting *he* was more popular with Halifax fans and by tossing long-stemmed roses to women as he strutted up the aisle to the ring.

"After I beat him," Downey recalls, "people threw the flowers back into the ring. Some of the thorns and things struck me while I'm in there celebratin' and all happy. *I thought they were throwin' them at me for beatin' him.* Really people were throwin' them back at him. I didn't know. I thought they were throwin' them out of disappointment."

Just 22 days later, Downey defended his Canadian middleweight title — his first defence since he had regained it from Gary Broughton 18 months before. The promoters — Ron Wallace, a Halifax MLA and future mayor, and Fred Bishop, the region's representative for *Ring* — further demonstrated the blurry demarcation between boxing, politics and journalism. Downey would receive $3000 for the fight.

His opponent was Joey Durelle.

The many wars of 'Joey Durable' were carved into a face that at once horrified and amused. The imprints of 61 professional fights merged with scars, lumps and crevasses resulting from disputes that took place outside a boxing ring. A cousin of New Brunswick legend Yvon Durelle, Joey inherited the pugnacious genes of the Baie Ste. Anne family that fought as a matter of course. "A *little* dirty?" laughs Halifax promoter Sonny MacPhee. "When you fought Joey Durelle, you won the fight, but after the fight he went to a dance and you went to a hospital."

Joey Durelle enjoyed being Joey Durelle. Summering in Baie Ste. Anne, a hard-luck fishing community of dirt roads and tarpapered houses, he would flaunt the trappings of his success — big car, sharp clothes and a grand ego. Always at the centre of the liveliest parties, Durelle liked to cook almost as much as he liked to flirt with the local women. "Down home there was a lot of boxers," according to a family friend. "You could tell they were a boxer by their deep voice, and the way they walked, and that they'd go around showing off their muscles. Joey was like that. He was always a bit of a macho man."

He had been a prizefighter since 1959. Between April 1968 and January 1970 he fought 18 times. There were 10 fights in 1960 alone. In 1964 he won the Canadian welterweight title, holding it until 1969, when he lost a decision — and then a rematch — to Montreal prodigy Donato Paduano. But decent credentials and a gift for juvenile pre-fight posturing could not camouflage the fact that by 1972 Durelle was a spent fighter.

Against Downey all doubt vanished at the opening bell. Up on his toes, Downey circled and repeatedly drilled jabs into Durelle's face. Picking his shots. Moving from the body to head with ease. Outpunching the flat-footed New Brunswicker ten-to-one, bruising the area around his left eye and cutting the bridge of his nose. Wrote Harris Sullivan, "Durelle, who claims to be 33, moved like he was carrying a piano on his back. [He] used to be a tough, mauling scrapper. He's lost his stuff."

After the decision was announced, Downey moved to the middle of the ring and reached for the microphone. The announcer recoiled and tightened his grip. A brief, embarrassing tug-of-war ensured. "Give it to him!" a disembodied voice screeched. "He's the champ!"

The announcer relented.

"Joey Durelle fought a good fight," Downey shouted as the crowd dwindled. He then again proclaimed he would fight more often, maybe even against media pet Paduano — a fight that would never take place. Finally, the middleweight champion of Canada said, "Halifax fans are the best fans in the world!"

His supporters cheered. Many others were already through the exits.

But if the crowds and the press remained cool to Downey, he still had friends in politics.

The press release from the office of Halifax mayor Walter Fitzgerald was contrite. "The committee which has organized Dave Downey Day quite properly has brought to our attention the fact that for the past five years a native-born Nova Scotian and Haligonian has held this national title, a feat which is accomplished by very few individuals. And yet, Dave Downey is virtually unknown to Haligonians. Therefore [I wish] to rectify this oversight and publicly pay tribute to Dave Downey for his outstanding feat which has brought much honour to our city and province."

Dave Downey Day, on Saturday, November 18, 1972, was as much about politics and black votes as boxing achievement. Certainly several local journalists wondered why there should even *be* a Dave Downey Day, given his habit of not fighting too often. No matter. The lengthy tribute demonstrated that Downey was an appealing figure in North End Halifax, with ample social grace.

In a half-page article in the *Chronicle-Herald* the day before, boxing writer Ken Jennex framed his subject as upbeat and humble, grateful for the honour and proud of his family. In the piece, Downey spoke of his mother: "No mother wants to see her son fight." He thanked entrepreneur Victor Beed for financing his trip to train in Boston for the Jimmy Meilleur fight: "I'm deeply indebted to him." He recalled his old neighbourhood: "The kids used to beat me around the neighbourhood." He stressed his obligation to his fans: "I always try to give the people my best." He even quoted Blair Richardson: "I know you're going to be the middleweight champ of Canada."

He also spoke of his four children — David Jr., 10, Delores, 7, Leotra, 6 and Raymond, 5 — offering an extra thought about his eldest. "He says he's going to be like me. He's going to find it tough, like I did."

The children had recently moved with their mother, Judy Gabriel, to Nova Scotia's South Shore when she and Downey had ended their decade-long common-law union. He would not have another serious relationship until he was in his mid-30s, with Helen Viner, a civil servant.

Dave Downey Day commenced in a mid-morning drizzle with the honouree meeting the mayor at Halifax City Hall. He then crossed the Angus L. MacDonald Bridge to Dartmouth City Hall where he was similarly greeted by Mayor Roland Thornhill. Next came gifts of cufflinks during appearances at the East Preston Centennial Centre and the Bayer's Road Shopping Centre in Halifax.

The afternoon featured a motorcade that crawled along Barrington and Gottingen streets as the grey clouds gave way to the sun. Dressed in a black fur coat, a black velvet suit and a large hat with a dipping brim, Downey, in a lead car, gratefully acknowledged everyone who stopped to gawk. The procession terminated at the Casino Theatre on Gottingen, where he received more cufflinks. A short time later he was introduced to the crowd during halftime at the Atlantic Bowl football game at Saint Mary's University. Along with a knot of tribute organizers he headed back downtown to Scotia Square and yet another presentation and still more cufflinks. At every point Downey conferred his appreciation and blazed his 1,000-megawatt smile.

More accolades poured forth that evening at a dinner before friends, family and second-line politicos in the banquet room of a hotel at the base of Citadel Hill. Gifts included a black-and-white television.

Nova Scotia premier Gerald Regan was represented by provincial secretary Garnet Brown who told how Downey and the premier had been "long and close friends and are in contact almost daily" through Downey's job at the Provincial Building.

Walter Fitzgerald was represented by Halifax's deputy mayor Dave MacKeen, who read a letter from Fitzgerald. It thanked

Downey for "having worn the mantle of champion with dignity, which reflects to the credit not only of the black people but of all the citizens of Halifax." MacKeen then added, "Dave has been a controversial champion but he's been a fighter and a winner."

Roland Thornhill was represented by Dartmouth's deputy mayor Frank Barber, who also paid homage.

Other benefactors included promoters Al Zinck and Jay Davis, who handed Downey a trophy, and Jules Oliver, representing the Black United Front, who unveiled a plaque in Downey's name to be awarded annually to the area's most promising amateur fighter.

And finally, a standing ovation.

"I would like to say thank you to everyone here for what you have done for me," the honouree told the assemblage.

Today Downey is reserved about the day-long veneration, cognizant now — as he was then — of its political hue. "That was after the second fight with Broughton, and so they wanted to do something. At least I had my family there and we all had a dinner, we all had a chance to mingle, and they all had a chance to speak and say something. If they were trying to make up some things [with me] ... maybe that's what they were trying to do."

The civic acknowledgement occurred in the middle of another dry period in Downey's boxing career. Following the easy win over Joey Durelle in June 1972, he would not fight again for another nine months. As usual, he continued to train.

For boxing in Halifax generally, 1973 was not a banner year. Promoters were reluctant to come forward for more than a one-shot effort, dissuaded by poor turnouts and bad publicity. Proffered Alex J. Walling in the *Scotian Journalist,* "Boxing in Halifax will be filed under the obituary column."

Some attempts were at least credible — a card that showcased promising welterweight Lawrence Hafey drew 1,500 customers. Others were downright wacky.

None more so than a Jay Davis promotion featuring heavyweight contender Alvin 'Blue' Lewis against Claude 'Humphrey' McBride, an Oklahoman behemoth in matching polka dot trunks and beret. Catcalls filled the Forum as the pair pawed at one another for a few rounds, after which McBride ran out of gas and flopped to the canvas. "A farce like this might be okay as a curtain raiser," wrote the *Chronicle-Herald's* Hugh Townsend. "As a main event, it's the type of thing that boxing can do without."

Into this void came two Nova Scotian promoters, one experienced, the other untried. Both constructed programs with Downey as the centrepiece. Both lost money.

Sydney-based Gussie MacLellan, who had promoted cards for three decades across the Maritimes, had been absent from the Halifax fight scene for almost a decade after being one of its central figures during the Kid Howard era. Sensing a vacuum in the city, he matched Downey with Tony Berrios, 24, from Scranton, Pennsylvania, who had lost his previous five fights. Downey–Berrios ended in a draw, but most observers felt Berrios won handily. Ken Jennex of the *Chronicle-Herald* called it "a clear-cut case of a hometown decision." Questionable judging also marred other bouts on the card.

Attendance was 1,236. MacLellan returned home to Sydney.

The other promoter to try his luck was Wayne Adams, who in 1992 would become Nova Scotia's first black cabinet minister. In 1973 he was best known for his Sunday night radio show on CHNS, *Black Journal*. Adam's card had a more engaging main event, with Downey earning a unanimous decision over a tall, tough 25-year-old from Cincinnati named Roy Dale. In Downey's corner was Tom McCluskey, who shrewdly insisted the boxer attack Dale with body shots. Downey heeded the advice. "If he would fight more often and put on that kind of display regularly, he could win back the many fans he has lost," observed Townsend, adding that Downey's comeback saved the lacklustre card.

In the same way that an opponent like Joe Frazier was vital to Muhammad Ali, so was Gary Broughton essential to David Downey.

In September 1973 the two fighters, near the end of their careers, headed toward their third and final meeting. Each grasped that the other man was his standard, enabling the boxing world —

and whatever passes for Canada's boxing history — to ultimately assign each his place.

Fate had supplied Downey with an intriguing soulmate. In a barbaric sport of early death and dark obsession, few men were more complex than Gary Broughton. "[I've] a lifestyle that is entirely and completely different than anybody else's," he once declared to the *Brantford Expositor.*

Few understood *how* different.

"I always found him to be very quiet, a gentleman," reflects May Bricker. "Well-spoken, well-educated. He was a loner. And he got more of a loner as he got older. He never seemed able to put down roots. Just one of those wandering spirits that you couldn't get close to, that you couldn't give advice to. Gary always seemed to be a lost soul. Lack of a friend, lack of a family. Sort of like an orphan. Never seemed to attach himself to anybody. Somehow you couldn't get close to him to try and help to do anything."

"The people that got to know him liked him," reflects Ron Craig, a friend in Brantford. "But they didn't really *know* him. I guess none of us really knew him."

Broughton was born in Pontefract, a market town near Leeds in Yorkshire, England. His family immigrated to Canada in 1948, when he was eight, settling in Cambridge, Ontario. He was impressed with his new setting. "I told my mother, 'This is God's country,' " recalls the boxer. His father, William, was a physiotherapist and chiropodist. ("He took out toenails," smiles Broughton.) Gary and his brother Mel, almost two years older, experienced a mostly pleasant childhood in a home that sometimes included foster children.

"My mother (Alice) was always vivacious, friendly, and in the house she was always singing," says Broughton. "She baked cookies and all kinds of stuff. Very much a housewife and a mother. Dad was happy, friendly, jovial but strict. Very old-fashioned, very military. In the Air Force in the Second World War, where he practised his therapy, he'd shine his shoes so he could see his face in them. Never used bad language. Very polite. He liked his cup of tea. Didn't drink or smoke."

Broughton's father died in 1962 of a heart attack, leaving Alice to make her own way. She seized the challenge and blossomed into an even more gregarious and flamboyant woman, who dated often, laughed loudly and wore flowing garments — at odds with the staid southern Ontario of the early 1960s. For a period she operated a grocery store downtown in Cambridge, and, with a new husband, launched a dance club for Kitchener's mature singles. She also owned a boutique in Kitchener where for a few hours each week Gary vacuumed, unwrapped new dresses and did rudimentary bookkeeping.

Once when his mother was ill he ran the boutique, dressing mannequins in a hot, enclosed display window in full view of the street and hating every minute of it. "I'd get the dresses on backwards sometimes."

At Preston High School in Cambridge, Broughton was an unmotivated and unremarkable student whose grades never reflected his intelligence. An avid reader, he became enamoured with literary masters, notably Somerset Maugham, whom Broughton abandoned when he learned Maugham was a 'bit crazy.' He failed Grade 13. "I couldn't study. My mind went. All I did was daydream, just daydream."

His interest in sports waned as well, although he had some natural gifts. "Most of the sports that he excelled in were individual sports," notes a former classmate. "He wasn't [a] team player."

Years later as a mature student he aborted an attempt to earn an English degree from Waterloo Lutheran University. "I couldn't be bothered with it."

As the indolent adolescent developed into the iconoclastic adult, Broughton drifted sluggishly in the manner that would characterize his life and baffle his acquaintances. While his boxing evolved, he took on a succession of jobs between fights to make ends meet. All were short-lived. He worked on construction sites, refilled food-dispensing machines, stacked trays in a bakery, assisted a bricklayer and tightened screws on an assembly line. "The longest I've ever had to work at one job since 1964 was six months," he boasted to the *Expositor.*

"Gary's not fond of work," May Bricker remembers thinking.

While around him others measured success in material terms, money neither concerned nor stimulated him. This was fortunate because his fight purses were embarrassingly meagre. "When I first turned pro," Broughton once told the *Kitchener-Waterloo Record,* "I got $50 for a four-rounder and $80 for a six-rounder. Hell, my expenses were more than the purse. I was virtually fighting for nothing, but the adventure and the achievement kept me going. It's the same as a person going on a Ferris wheel. He does it for the thrill."

At mid-career he was drawing only about $150 a fight. Twice he earned just $60. Part-time jobs boosted his annual income to about $6,000, enough to sustain a lifestyle that included a long period at the Brantford YMCA. Ron Craig, who as a young $100-a-week newspaper reporter also lived at the Y, recalls, "[The rooms were] like cells. No toilets, just a bed, clothes closet, a table, a washroom with shower stalls in there. In those days, it was seven dollars a week. We ate out, but they served evening meals at the Y for a dollar."

Craig and Broughton became chums. This meant bass fishing occasionally and drinking together frequently. Craig remembers a well-read, worldly, informed — even eloquent — friend who was easy to talk with, but who drank like there was no tomorrow. "He was a great quipster. He could come back with the parry-and-thrust with everyday guys. He was right in the centre of it. He gave as good as he got, maybe better. He was a really sharp guy, no doubt about it. He was on a higher plane than most people."

The tavern was Broughton's preferred forum to display his intellect. He patronized several. "He drank a lot — a lot!" says Craig. "I was usually drunk right along with him, so I can't recount much of the detail. The hotel was right across from the newspaper, so we just walked right across the parking lot and we were there. Whatever the occasion. And if there wasn't one, we made one up."

From time to time his drinking led to confrontations. Although Broughton seldom instigated, he was frequently targeted by drunken goons hankering to take on a pro. Such battles were doubly precarious for Broughton. As a prizefighter he was in a legal dilemma should he seriously hurt anyone, plus he risked damaging his own hands, which he did several times anyway.

"If I had my back to the wall in a dark alley and saw some rough guys coming my way, the one man I'd want beside me would be Gary Broughton," one friend offers.

Craig remembers one early-morning incident outside the Brantford YMCA. "It was after a lacrosse game and there were three fellas that were carryin' on and Broughton was walking down the street with two of his friends. One of his friends said something to these guys and the guys went around the block and then came back in a car. They jumped out of the car — three of them — and Broughton is standing there. And his two friends ran into the Y! Those two friends came back out after two of the guys were [lying] on the sidewalk. They [the three strangers] had no idea who [Gary] was. It was just bang-bang! And he loved it! If there was someone who was stupid enough to take him on, he was more than happy to accommodate him."

He claims to have had about 30 street fights, starting in his mid-teens when he was scrawny and older kids pushed him around. Once in a hotel he bumped into a man who elected to turn the accident into an incident. "This fellow — he was six-foot-four — grabbed me and said, 'Watch where you are goin'!' And I said, 'Get your hands off me!' I was drunk. I swung and I managed to break his cheekbone. He had 23 stitches in his eyebrows. I was charged with assault. This would be '68. Frank [Bricker] wasn't mad. He just shook his head and said, 'Gotta stop drinkin', Gary.' "

He was convicted but got probation, not jail time.

In boxing Broughton found his *métier,* his anchor. The sport established parameters and became his means of self-expression. It was the lone endeavour that bestowed a feeling of accomplishment. "Boxing has given me a single-mindedness," he proclaimed late in his career. "There's nothing to compare with the loneliness you find inside the ring. It enables me to meet other situations where you have to be independent. When I first started boxing as an amateur I was shy and timid, not forceful. Now I feel that I'm an aggressive person."

Such capacity for self-analysis charmed newspaper reporters, already predisposed to admire anyone who fought so often and so hard. Reporters also lauded his commitment to physical fitness — he claimed to run three and a half miles daily — apparently unconcerned that sweat was increasingly offset by alcohol.

"I started drinking when I was 15 years old. The first time I took a shot of rye whiskey I felt 10 feet tall and eight feet wide. I thought in the back of my mind, 'I got to get more of that.' " Drinking initially affected his studies in high school. Later it made it difficult for him to keep a job. "Sometimes I would get so drunk that I'd forget what day it was and I wouldn't show up for work and they would fire me. Just as simple as that."

Drunk "six or seven days a week," he'd dry out four days or so before the fights. He asserts he never fought when he was drunk.

Booze was not his only issue. At the crest of his career, rumours swirled concerning his sexual preference. Brantford's tiny boxing circle held that he was either homosexual or bisexual. Whispers soon spread to other centres, including Halifax.

"Fabrication," Broughton asserts. "They are wrong." Anyone who would conclude that would be guessing, he smiles. "People make up silly stories."

In the early 1970s, with those rumours in full flower, Broughton would overtly stress his attraction to women. He told the *Chronicle-Herald,* "I was engaged at one point, but my girlfriend worried about me all the time. I told her boxing was my life, so it ended there.

"Sometimes I get lonely," he added. "I like girls."

Today Broughton grins as he recalls his quest for women. "At the Kress Hotel, at the Graham Bell Hotel, oh the girls were wonderful. They'd take my breath away. I'd just stare at them — wow! If I got lucky, then I'd get lucky."

He says he had significant relationships through the years with six different women, a level of activity corroborated by his friend Ron Craig. "He chased women just as vigorously as anyone I've ever met. And when he caught them, I'm sure he knew what to do." Whatever the reason, his relationships with women didn't last. Craig remembers him crying in his room at the Y after an attractive blond girl turned him down.

Broughton maintains that personal relationships were usually scuttled by the absolute focus that boxing mandated. Another factor was the sport's stark manifestation. "It's hard on a woman for a fellow to come home with his nose broken, a black eye and tooth knocked out."

And then there was that other thing. "They all got worried about me drinking. They all said the same thing, 'I can't take it any longer. You're always drunk.' "

The instruction sheet for Gary Broughton's career appeared to consist of a solitary word — fight. After losing the Canadian middleweight title to Downey in December 1970, he had won nine, lost five and drew once. Many were brutal engagements for minuscule pay. Three matches in 1973, all before his final showdown that year with Downey, were typical of the frantic strategy of a mercenary.

In Philadelphia, Bobby 'Boogaloo' Watts, a top contender who had beaten 'Marvelous' Marvin Hagler, was twice staggered by Broughton, but recovered to take a 10-round decision. The defeat netted Broughton $700 (after expenses), along with a deep gash inside his mouth. "He swallowed a lot of blood," observed Frank Bricker.

In Halifax, Joey Durelle and Broughton hammered one another into exhaustion for 10 rounds in a clumsy contest won by Broughton. Both bled from cuts over their eyes, their faces reddened and swollen.

Also in Halifax, Broughton knocked out Irish Mike Baker, 21, *The Ring's* top prospect of 1973. The upset stirred interest in a third fight with Downey. "Downey's brother was at the press conference after the fight," Broughton informed the *Kitchener-Waterloo Record.*

"I told him that if Dave wants to make a little money, I'm his candy-man."

11

RECKONING

The middleweight championship of Canada put little food on David Downey's table, but it nourished his ego well.

Newspapers printed his name. Strangers pointed when he strolled through shopping malls. Friends waved as he tooled around the North End behind the wheel of brother Billy's metallic gold Cadillac.

David Downey and Vince Hennebury with some North End youngsters.

He says his four children felt it too, in their school and around their neighbourhood. "People used to come and tell them, 'you're David's daughter,' 'you're David's son.' "

"That would happen all the time," says Delores, the eldest daughter. "I would just smile and say, 'Yup, that's my dad.' " Some even assumed Delores and her younger sister, Leotra, knew how to fight. "And I can't fight a lick!"

Neither ever saw their father in an actual prizefight, but they recall that boxing was a big part of his life. Sometimes they accompanied him to the gym as he helped train his nephews. Delores remembers watching televised fights together with her dad. As youngsters the two girls and their two brothers moved with their mother, Judy Gabriel, to Yarmouth, Nova Scotia, 200 miles from Halifax. Downey visited them three or four times a year and made frequent phone calls, say the daughters, now in their 40s. They affirm both their mother and father insisted on respect for elders, just as David's parents did in his youth.

"Sometimes he'd get on our case, even over the phone," says Leotra. "He was always there for us. He would call us. We would call him. He would come down to surprise us and we'd go up to Halifax to surprise him.

"We never had to worry about someone else being our dad. *He* was our dad."

"My kids and me always enjoyed good relationships," says Downey. "Always. I loved being able to share my wins with them. I'd go shopping. I did everything that a dad would probably do. At that time, when I was winning, those kids had just as much as any kid around here. It added meaning to my accomplishments. They could say that 'my dad was the champ'."

While the government of Nova Scotia paid him to move office furniture or spend days in a downtown parking booth, the championship granted Downey a realm all his own, where *he* controlled events, where only the views that aligned with *his* needed to be observed. Alone, the title made him exceptional. Even if others — especially media types — did not feel the glow.

As he prepared to meet Broughton for the third time, Downey

could not forget the sense of dislocation that followed his setback in 1970 at their first meeting, when he lost the title. So for their third fight, the decisive encounter, he would leave nothing to chance. With another leave-of-absence from his job, Downey traced the familiar pattern and headed south to the States. This time it was to New York and George Gainford, who counselled — or attempted to counsel — the obstinate Sugar Ray Robinson in his prime. Downey's sessions with Gainford were gruelling, as exacting as any in his 13 years as a prizefighter. But he did not complain, even as the experience drained him and turned his demeanour raw.

The rigour of the camp was offset by the people who wove through his days. New York people. Real fight people, prepared to extol his boxing endowments. They talked about him having a shot at the British Commonwealth title. Maybe even the world title. An easy warm-up victory in Oklahoma City over an American named Tony Gardner boosted the dream. In the flame of such lofty possibilities, Downey savoured the respect and prepared for The Brantford Bomber.

The penultimate chapters of two peculiar boxing careers would be written at the Halifax Forum on September 27, 1973, an occasion tagged the 'Night of Champions.' According to its neophyte promoter Bill Hartlen — who occasionally contributed cash to Downey's cause through the years — the Downey–Broughton showdown, the centrepiece of the evening, was the reckoning "everyone has been waiting to see."

Hartlen was best known for operating local concessions. He did especially brisk trade in the canteen beneath Section 6 on the Forum's south side, dispensing greasy foodstuffs that would lull the taste buds of two generations of Haligonians. Immediately following major sports events — and many not-so-major events — Hartlen would host favoured journalists and a gaggle of Forum regulars to lobster, deer steak, booze and the like.

"He was hidin' all the money," insists Murray Sleep. "When he died, [the] income tax started investigating. They went down the basement [of his house] and found thousands and thousands and thousands of dollars. Did he skim! But he wasn't a promoter. If someone came to him and said 'Bill, we're lookin' for a promoter to put a fight on here at the Forum, and you're gonna benefit too' — which he would by sellin' hot dogs and burgers — Bill would go for it if it wasn't too expensive. But he wasn't a promoter."

Regardless, he was doing nicely for a pretender. Earlier in the year he had presented the card that featured Broughton against Irish Mike Baker. Although only 1,300 fans attended, Alex J. Walling declared in the alternative press that Hartlen's effort "may have saved Halifax as a boxing city."

Now in the late summer of 1973, along with New York fight man Jay Davis, Hartlen was promoting again. And again doing it relatively well, if advance ticket sales of $7,000 were any measure of success. This virtually ensured that the venture — with many past and present Canadian titleholders on hand to be part of the show in some manner — would at least break even.

Unquestionably there was a legitimate public thirst to see Downey and Broughton settle their series.

And both fighters adroitly contributed to the sense of the moment.

In interviews Broughton seemed reasonable and candid, devoid of the braggadocio that made prizefighting increasingly sound like a brassy and brainless offshoot of the B-grade entertainment industry. Broughton pointed out that since their last meeting he had fought 15 times and Downey just three. "I'm bound to be in better condition," he told Ted Beare, of the *Brantford Expositor.* "I'm bound to have improved."

In their two previous meetings he had chased Downey around the ring, missing punches and tiring himself needlessly. Now he promised to attack more intelligently, more strategically, and shrink the ring by angling Downey into corners while seeking to land the decisive bomb. "Maybe I'm a little slower than I was three years ago, but I'm smarter, I'm a better fighter and I'm stronger."

Although he was highly suspicious of the media, Downey also co-operated, a marked "reversal from previous occasions", noted *Chronicle-Herald* columnist Hugh Townsend.

Downey told the *Herald's* Ken Jennex, "I'll beat him with the greatest of ease. After the second or third rounds there will be no doubt in the people's minds as to who is going to dominate the fight. The people are going to get sick of seeing me hitting him."

In a television interview the day before the fight, he confessed for the first time publicly that the jeering from Halifax fans troubled and disappointed him. "I'm a Halifax guy and I want to fight here in my hometown. It hurts to hear that stuff."

The Halifax Forum filled rapidly on the Night of Champions. As cigarette smoke collected leisurely above the ring, the familiar checkerboard began to appear as black and white patrons arranged in distinct blocks. Racial tension in the city had eased slightly over the last year or so, but blacks still had fewer jobs, less income and more police attention. And all remembered the explosion that followed the first Downey–Broughton clash three years before. While some dismissed the third fight's social significance, boxing has always thrived on ethnic confrontation.

And Downey was still black. Broughton was still white.

Downey–Broughton attracted attention beyond Nova Scotia. Upper Canadian newspapers actually acknowledged the fight, and it enticed at least one major international boxing figure to the Forum. But those who knew Bill Brennan and boxing's inner order took little comfort in the presence of a man rumoured to be closely linked with the sport's underbelly.

Brennan, of Richmond, Virginia, was chairman of the World Boxing Association ratings committee and a WBA past president. He first visited Halifax in the late 1950s as a petty officer in the U.S. Navy. Upon his return in September 1973 he discovered a town that appeared to still care about boxing.

Brennan arrived a few days before Downey–Broughton, pronouncing the sport "in excellent shape" worldwide, even as studies continued to show that cerebral damage in veteran fighters was pervasive. At the Forum on fight night he was accompanied by Chris Cline, the Washington-based manager of the highly aggrieved Doc Holliday. Just one year before, Cline had departed Halifax with his fighter, ranting that Downey would never fight again. Now the same Cline, obviously prepared to let bygones be bygones for the good of this noble pastime, cosied up to his pal Brennan.

Together they sniffed the scent of money. Not big money — this was Halifax, Nova Scotia, after all — but a sweet fragrance uncommon in all but the heavyweight division. Brennan seemed delighted to be part of it all. So happy, in fact, that he was eager to offer advice to those guiding the sport in this northern backwater. "I'll gladly discuss boxing problems of any nature with them," he told the *Chronicle-Herald*.

The instant Downey appeared through the small entranceway, he was met with an overture of derision that swelled as he neared the ring. Boos, catcalls, insults. "Growling belches of disapproval," Harris Sullivan would later write. Downey heard each one. Fight after fight, since he had won his title six years before, the reception grew steadily more negative. But never before had it been this impassioned, this spiteful.

Surrounding the 31-year-old champion was the usual local cast, plus a few New Yorkers who in recent weeks had helped train him. Towards the ring he bounced, lowering his hands to his side and twisting his torso to steady the nerves. Focused. Proud. Wounded. Observed Sullivan in the *4th Estate*, "[There] was no warmth for Downey. Here was this handsome Halifax fighter defending his Canadian title in his hometown and he was greeted if he were the enemy."

He jogged up the steps, sprang over the top rope, and performed his customary mid-air splits, ignoring Broughton who had been waiting for several minutes in the ring, the hood of his metallic green robe pulled down over his head. Broughton too was bouncing lightly, his gaze fixed on his opponent as Frank Bricker recited the customary pre-fight cant.

Ring announcer Johnny Fortunato watched Downey's entrance, then waited until the reaction subsided. In his flat-edged Boston accent, Fortunato, in keeping with the evening's promotional theme, began to acknowledge the parade of 'champion' pugilists squeezing through the ropes.

"Art Hafey!" — Loud cheers.

"Dickie 'Kid' Howard!" — A standing ovation.

"Donato Paduano!" — Cheers, whistles, some boos.

"Clyde Gray!" — Thunderous cheering.

For Gray, the native son who settled in Hogtown and won the Commonwealth welterweight championship, there seemed no racial chasm. He nodded and waved to the crowd. He then skipped across to grip the gloves of Broughton and Downey. Moved by the tribute, he waved a second time. This relaunched the cheering and Gray acknowledged it yet again.

At the press table Hugh Townsend surveyed the ceremony and permitted his thoughts to drift. "[As] I looked into the ring," he wrote in his column the next morning, "viewing three Nova Scotians who are tops in Canada in their respective weight divisions and a fourth who was a Canadian champ, I couldn't help but think of a man who wasn't there for this great night. The late Blair Richardson, my favourite throughout his colourful career as middleweight king, would have stood tall among the many other dignitaries inside the ropes." (Richardson died of a brain tumour in 1971. His early death was not officially linked to boxing.)

Meanwhile Downey bounced in his corner, consenting to the ritual of extending his gloves to greet the brethren as they approached him one by one. At least the boos had stopped for a while.

Fortunato introduced the main event fighters. Downey's reception was mixed. Broughton was cheered loudly. Downey continued to prance and punch as if he didn't give a damn.

Then Downey peeled back his robe. His riposte. Four thousand pairs of eyes riveted to 159 pounds of spring-tight sinew that proclaimed every New York sit-up, push-up and sparring session. His lanky opponent across the ring — at least seven pounds lighter and looking pale, weedy and vulnerable — was about to suffer for every jeer and catcall directed at Downey that night and every night for the last six years.

The fighters walked to the centre of the ring.

"You lock on him," says Downey of his technique at such moments. "I always looked at their face. Not for a staredown, I look at their face [for] any scar at all on them. If you hit scar tissue long enough, it'll open. And you're looking to see if he's afraid of you."

It was 10:40 pm.

The assault was instant and unforgiving. Downey darted across the ring and connected with two sharp jabs and sundry other blows. The siege made Broughton step back to regain his balance, to try to locate his opponent. When he finally did, he encountered more jabs and more hooks that, according to the *Chronicle-Herald's* Ken Jennex, "had Broughton's head snapping back and forth as if his neck were on string." In the second round, Downey swatted Broughton's head with such force that vibrations pulsed down his own torso, prompting him to back off and shake his hand a few times to determine if it was seriously hurt. It wasn't.

His aggression persisted through the third. Gradually the booing subsided. Remarkably by the middle rounds most of the Forum was now cheering Downey. He continued to press. At the end of the sixth, Broughton returned to his corner with blood trickling from cuts along the left eyebrow and under his lower lip. His nose also bled. The Brantford Bomber spat blood as he flopped on his stool, his eyes lifeless.

"Downey showed total disregard for Broughton's punching ability," wrote Jennex, "and any time Broughton managed to connect, which was seldom, he only managed to increase the intensity of Downey's attack. Downey's fantastic performance opened another cut, this time under Broughton left eye, in the ninth round."

Exploiting his weight advantage, Downey bulled the challenger into the ropes and trapped him in the corners — the very thing Broughton planned to do to Downey. In the first two fights it was in such quarters that Broughton had his best moments. On this night, Downey's power overwhelmed him, even in close.

Broughton's attack was leaden. His timing erratic, he pawed some jabs and a few rights, but nothing broke Downey's resolve or rhythm. Murray Sleep, who has witnessed hundreds of matches, today believes it was the worst beating he ever saw one prizefighter give another.

Hundreds began chanting, "Go Dave go." Through it all, Gary Broughton stood bloody, overmatched, refusing to fall. Not once. Downey continued. Jabs, hooks, more jabs, crosses. "[A] human punching machine," noted Jennex.

Then in the eleventh and twelfth rounds — a huge public relations mistake. Downey began to mock Broughton by dropping his gloves and motioning him forward, taunting the beaten athlete. Such displays were becoming familiar in American rings, but in the embattled, racially strained Halifax of the1970s, mockery did not sit well. The cheering for Downey stopped as suddenly as it had begun.

"The depth of the dislike for Downey surfaced in the last rounds," reported Sullivan, "when the champ, knowing he was in command and wanting to bask in the flash of it all, began doing a little dance instead of throwing punches at the frustrated and beaten Broughton. Back came the jeers, ugly and angry. No, it was going to take more than one good show by Downey to win over the detractors."

Hugh Townsend scored the fight 12-0-0. "It was truly a different-looking Downey in the ring," he wrote the next day. "He was mean, he was a tiger, he attacked Broughton from the opening bell."

The real judges were only a little less generous. John Sansom 11-0-1, Stu Isnor 8-3-1, James Greig 10-0-2. "[Isnor] gave Broughton three rounds," scoffed Sullivan in the *4th Estate*, "but he was watching something else or wanted to soothe the wounds of a nice man from England, or else he wished to show that he should be judging beauty contests, or wrestling matches or some other sideshow."

Broughton walked unaided to his dressing room where his manager attempted to explain the evening. Maybe Gary did a little too much running. He had tonsillitis a few weeks before. He had fought three or four tough fights in a row. Maybe it was a combination of all these things. In any case a good rest is in order. At least until after Christmas. "He seemed a little weak," said Frank Bricker.

In post-fight interviews Broughton, too, would offer up over-training, tonsillitis and the like. But another reason went unspoken — Broughton had mistimed his booze.

"In between fights," Broughton now explains, "[I'd start to dry out] three or four days before the fights. I drank after each workout. That was the pattern. I couldn't stop. I might have to have a couple of beers the day before to deal with the withdrawal symptom. It's low blood sugar. You'd get so tired that you'd lose the boxing match. So I'd have to have a few drinks sometime just as the boxing match came close."

Broughton remembers he did not "refuel" before his third Downey fight. He says that consequently his blood sugar was very low. He postulates this is why he had so little energy. "I wasn't well. My alcoholism was progressing. I weighed 152 pounds. I was drinking, I was getting older and the illness was progressing. I was losing weight when I should have been gaining weight."

A little after midnight, looking in his own words like "a leftover from the Halifax explosion," Broughton strolled into the Lobster Trap, a popular downtown Halifax nightclub. Patrons twisted to gawk at the battered contender whose broken nose had already turned a sickly yellow. Blood crusted near a v-shaped cut beneath his lower lip. His left eye was puffed and red.

"That's Broughton!" proclaimed one young man as the warrior entered. "That's the guy who fought Downey tonight." Several customers ventured to Broughton's table and shook his hand. Strangers he'd met *en route* to the club had extended a similar welcome.

"You know why I'm popular down here?" Broughton gloated to his friend and *Kitchener-Waterloo Record* reporter Tom Conway. "I'm their kind of fighter. I'm a working man's fighter. I don't win all the time, so they can identify with me. If you're good at something or you win all the time, people resent it. They don't like someone who always wins.

"I'm not the kind to brood about things. What's past is past. I have no grudge against Downey. I knocked him out to win the title, he won it back, and now he's beaten me again. So what! If I harboured grudges against every guy I lost to, I'd be a bitter guy.

"I lost, but they love me down here."

As for Downey, Broughton doubted he'd follow through on his commitment to fight more frequently. "He just doesn't like fighting. It takes too much discipline. He'll probably fight Paduano, but then there'll be another long period of drought. Though who knows? Maybe I've motivated him."

A few blocks away in the Arrows Club, Downey, whose face was unmarked, was also receiving congratulations from admirers, both black and white. But his victory felt tarnished by the hostility of the hometown crowd.

"I wish they wouldn't boo me," the Canadian middleweight champion told Harris Sullivan over the din. "It's home and I wanted to please these fans.

"I wish they wouldn't boo me."

12

PROSPECT

As an amateur and young professional, Lawrence Hafey was often called a 'prospect'. The label inspired him as he'd trek seven miles from a modest home in the Lourdes section of Stellarton, Nova Scotia, to the Archie Moore Boxing Club on the Pictou Landing Road. There, in the mid-1960s, he would spar, pound the heavy bag and do hundreds of sit-ups because older men who growled the argot of the craft insisted this is what prospects do. For two, three or four hours. Every day. Then he would shower and walk the seven miles back home.

As a pro welterweight he won 14 of his first 20 matches. Soon, however, he ran up against other prospects and cunning veterans who exposed his flaws and humbled his reputation. But at least no one could knock him off his feet.

By May 1975, when he faced David Downey for the middleweight title of Canada, few still called Lawrence Hafey 'A Prospect.'

He twice fought for the Canadian lightweight title, losing both times. He also took on two world-ranked fighters — Wilfredo Benitez and Bruno Arcari — and lost to both of those, too. At one point he moved to California but soon returned to Stellarton, where a fading wunderkind could feel more comfortable.

"That [Downey–Hafey] fight," says Doug Saunders, "even in its lead-up, became a black–white fight. Lawrence Hafey was polite about it. As far as he was concerned, Dave Downey was just another opponent. Dave Downey was polite. As far as he was concerned Lawrence Hafey was just another opponent. But somehow through the camps, or through society or whatever, it became a black-white fight. The old Halifax Forum that night, you could feel the electricity in the air. It was, 'Kill that black bastard' coming from about 50 percent of the people. It was, 'Kill that white sonofabitch' coming from the other 50 percent."

There were few secrets between Hafey and Downey. Hafey, 26, had 39 wins in 53 fights and had participated in numerous Forum cards over the years, including some featuring Downey. One major difference between the two men was their recent level of activity. This would be Hafey's 10th bout in 12 months, and his first as a middleweight. Downey had fought only twice in the 21 months since beating Gary Broughton in their third match. Both fights were wins — Dave Wyatt in Dayton, Ohio, in November 1973, and Newfoundlander Terry Hayward in Halifax in March 1974. The latter was a title defence.

Downey prepared for Hafey at the Halifax recreation department facility, assisted by a well-travelled local trainer named Ossie Meikle, a lightweight in the 1930s and 1940s. "For Downey, it's an old story," wrote Ace Foley, an authority on old stories, "a long period of inactivity then a sudden plunge back into the ring. This time the fans know the kind of opposition that he'll be facing and they seem to like the thoughts of an aggressive and durable challenger."

Hafey divided an exhaustive training schedule — he sparred 116 rounds — between Halifax and Ottawa. During one session alone, a few days before the match, he sparred 13 rounds. At some point he bruised his ribs badly. Hafey's manager Gerry Fraser and commission chairman Don Kerr both refuted a rumour that the injury would jeopardize the fight. Yet, on the night of the fight, as the card worked through its preliminaries, a minion representing promoters Gussie MacLellan and Alva Brown entered Downey's dressing room and announced that Hafey was indeed hurt. He said the main event *might* be called off.

Downey was stunned.

"You train for a fight, you are ready to fight. You're sittin' there and you're all dressed and they are out there tryin' to get someone to fight me? Anybody else might have just walked out of there and said, 'The hell with it. I want my money now! You made me wait.'"

About 20 minutes later Downey, now befuddled and agitated, was told that the fight would go ahead as planned.

The match itself was not exciting — "a fistic flop," columnist Hugh Townsend would write the next day. "All the hoopla, all the advance promise of a classic, all the drama and excitement that built into a fever pitch as the defending king and his challenger stepped through the ropes came to a crashing halt the moment the opening bell sounded. The 'battle' fell flat on its face, landing with a thud on the ring apron."

More than 6,000 watched Downey and Hafey cram and clinch rather than set and throw. Both unleashed kidney and rabbit punches, along with other cheap shots. Boos accompanied the end of most rounds. Referee Herb McMullan cautioned both men, scolding them between rounds for their listlessness. It all made the fight difficult to score.

"I'd go to throw a punch, he'd clinch me and hold me," recalls Downey, who weighed 160 pounds compared with Hafey's appreciably lighter 147. "I'd try to push him off. I told Herbie that I'm going to throw him out of the ring. Herb said, 'I'll disqualify you.' I said, 'Hell, you're gonna disqualify me anyway.' "

The fighters embraced at the final bell, Hafey's face revealing the battle far more than Downey's. As most spectators passively awaited the judges' decision, a clutch of Downey supporters, anticipating a Hafey verdict, began screaming that the outcome was fixed.

The fuse was lit.

Doug Saunders, who covered Hafey–Downey for local CBC television, was the first press man in the ring that night, hoping to harvest the passion before the decision was announced. Others soon arrived, including Bob Jones, a big CBC cameraman, Alex J. Walling of CHNS and many peeved Downey partisans.

"You don't interview a guy in the damn dressing room," says Saunders, "You interview him right after the fight is over. You capture the moment when he's still nine miles high and covered in sweat or blood and his emotions are running wild and the adrenaline's pumping."

The Forum quieted as announcer Johnny Fortunato pushed to ring centre and clutched the microphone as it plumed from the rafters. From the middle of the congestion Fortunato informed the Forum that one judge favoured Downey — but two favoured Hafey. All three judges were white.

"It was a very close fight," affirms Saunders. "But Lawrence Hafey won the fight. We went into the ring to interview Dave Downey, Walling and I. Me with my cameraman, and Alex with just his cassette recorder. And before we could even get to Dave Downey we were physically accosted by what I could only describe as a mob of black Downey supporters who felt their man had been jobbed.

"The decision hadn't even been rendered by the public address announcer yet and they were already demanding to know. They had me by the lapels — I had a sports jacket on and shirt and tie — shaking me: 'Who won the fight? Who won the fight?' "

When Fortunato announced Hafey had won "it was absolute pandemonium in the ring. I feared for my safety and I think Alex did as well. I remember him screaming and shouting at these guys as they physically accosted me to get their bloody hands off me, to leave me alone, to let me do my job."

Walling recalls Downey's corner erupted and the whole entourage began yelling, Fuckin' white trash! We was robbed! Goddamned white decision! We got robbed! "I never realized how much that middleweight championship of Canada, *of Canada!* — that no one other than the people of Halifax would even know about — meant to some of these people."

Among those in the ring was Bubby Adams, a sailor and a lifelong friend of Downey's. "We had heard that they were tryin' to get the title away from David for years. They had an idea that we weren't defending it enough and they wanted to give it to Lawrence Hafey. They were saying if it was close, they were just goin' to take the title away from David."

Adams, who is black, and a former boxer, says a sense of the imminent decision started circulating through the stands almost from the opening bell. At the announcement, Adams and about 15 buddies climbed into the ring and "got into a little problem with Lawrence Hafey's handlers."

Adams blamed frustration — "they were cheatin' him right there in front of our eyes" — not liquor for the battles that broke out. Indeed the clashes did not all follow racial lines. "There were a lot of black guys fightin' white guys, and white guys fightin' black guys, and white guys fightin' white guys, and black guys fightin' black guys."

Amid the chaos Downey and Hafey were escorted back to their dressing rooms.

Neither Saunders nor Walling were able to interview Downey in the ring. However, Walling's tape recorder was operating the entire time, capturing expletive-laced material he later used on his Sunday night radio show. Saunders refused to return to his television studio without questioning the fallen champion, so he took a deep breath and pressed down the aisle towards Downey's dressing room, not realizing that many of Downey's supporters had rounded the corner ahead of him.

"This same mob was standing barring his dressing room door. They asked me what I was doing there. I said I wanted to go in and interview Dave Downey. Three or four of them, particularly this Randy Braithwaite, said, 'You think he lost the fight?' I said, 'Yes I do.' And Randy started to take off his jacket. He was gonna have into me right then and there. And the others, my guess would have been 15 to 30 — I certainly didn't take a headcount, all started to scream. 'Kick the shit out of him! Kill the motherfucker!' Randy was right in my face."

Suddenly the dressing room door banged open.

There stood Downey.

In his white robe, his hands still taped, drenched in sweat, brow furrowed. He paused to take in the scene. "Leave him alone!" he screamed. "Let him in here! I want to talk to him! He's a friend of mine!"

Braithwaite and the others backed away from Saunders. Shouts for blood stopped. The young CBC reporter — ashen and trembling —

Election night 1974: Graham Downey (second from right) with David (far right). In the upper left is boxing promoter LeRoy 'Rocco' Jones.

darted past Downey into the dressing room. His cameraman followed closely. The dressing room door slammed behind them.

"Holy fuck!" gasped Saunders. "Why do they act like that?"

"I don't know," answered Downey. "I wonder, too."

Composing himself, Saunders thanked his liberator, uncurled his lapels, placed the microphone a few inches beneath Downey's chin and began the interview. When it finished, the fighter personally escorted Saunders and his cameraman to the Forum's main exit, still in his white robe, his fists still taped. A few cops hovered nearby.

Saunders soon met up with Walling, who had remained in the building to wait for his friend. He drove Saunders home, running at least one red light on the way. "I've been to the Canada–Russia series," says Walling, "I've been to Grey Cups, and a lot of things that rank incredibly high in terms of memorable moments, but *that* ...."

The incident generated at least one other memorable moment for Walling. It happened a few days later on his open-line show and commenced with the show's first call.

"Alex, what did you think of the fight's decision?' the voice on the line asked.

"Well, it was very close," replied Walling.

"Do you think Dave should get a rematch?"

"Yep, in a year and a half. Let him wait as long as he's made other people wait! Here's a guy who made the number one guy (Johan Louw) wait so long that he retired. Downey only offered him a chance *after* he retired." Walling needed a police escort to leave the radio station that night. "I had a bunch of people come to Tobin Street — a bunch of people who wanted to kill the open-line host! [My] producer said there were a couple of cars and that they wanted to 'talk' to me."

"I can only give you my opinion why all this happened," reflects Saunders, more than a quarter of a century later. "To [black people in Halifax] it was another example of another prominent black person having been screwed by white society. They honestly believed that Dave Downey had won the fight. They believed he had been robbed by Lawrence Hafey, by me, by Alex J. Walling, by the City of Halifax, by God — you name it."

Saunders was back on speaking terms with his would-be assailants within days, reminding them he wasn't a judge, but hearing yet again that the fact he was white and that the fact he was in the media meant he influenced the outcome of the fight. With that, the incident was dropped.

"I got the impression, because they never did bring it up again, that it was something that they weren't particularly proud of," says Saunders.

Downey admitted it was not a good fight. He also realized it *was* close. But boxing convention dictates close fights go to the champion, especially in the champion's hometown. So the judges should have tilted his way, Downey reasoned. He felt in his bones that the Canadian Professional Boxing Federation wanted another champion and somehow influenced the judges.

That's what those near him were alleging, too.

At least one member of the media shared Downey's perspective and his suspicion.

Gerry Fogarty began his CBC Radio sportscast the next morning this way: *If you are driving along Windsor Street right about now and you detect a very unpleasant odour, it's the one coming out of the Halifax Forum.*

"I think they took the title from Downey that night because they wanted someone else to occupy the position of Canadian middleweight champion," Fogarty says, rejecting the premise of a race-based decision. "They *took* his title that night. He didn't lose it in the ring. He just didn't fight [often] enough. He just didn't keep the sport alive the way boxing promoters and those who loved boxing wanted.

"Downey was someone you couldn't control. He was his own man in that sense. And I think they felt if they had another champion from Nova Scotia, they'd be able to promote more cards and have more title fights right here in Halifax."

For Downey, the evening's consternation began early when, between matches, he heard his two nephews jeered when they were presented to the crowd. "They've been representing the city, and a Downey won a silver medal at the Canada Winter Games. What more do they want?" he later complained to the *Chronicle-Herald*.

"They just don't like Downeys here."

Graham Downey had reason to think otherwise.

As David focused on Lawrence Hafey, Graham, three years David's senior, became the first black ever elected to Halifax city council. It took three tries.

Ward 3 was Halifax's core district and included the downtown and some older residential sections. Much of it was badly deteriorated. Three years before, Graham Downey had lost badly to David MacKeen, who was now running for mayor. In the 1974 election, Ward 3 was wide open, and an eclectic field of five seized the opportunity. It included Downey, a CBC stage designer; George West, an engineer and former city works director; and Frank Fillmore, the passionate but erratic journalist and publisher of the alternative the *Scotian Journalist.*

Downey's platform called for better housing, lighting and recreation facilities as well as cleaner streets, improved security, and lower rents. He was not a press favourite. The *4th Estate* called him inarticulate, unpopular and weak on the issues. The *Chronicle-Herald* endorsed West.

On election night Ward 3 was extraordinarily close. Initial results had Downey third, prompting many of his campaign workers to glumly leave his Gottingen Street headquarters. When a recount was announced many scurried back as the night continued. In the end, he collected 676 votes, just 15 more than Best and 21 ahead of Fillmore.

Downey went on to win the next eight elections, a record of continuity unsurpassed in the city's history. His family was engaged in every campaign.

Graham Downey's political breakthrough was helped by many factors. One was his association with the trendy Arrows Club. Another was the name recognition supplied by David's boxing success. Family connections with the provincial Liberal party didn't hurt either. And the local civil rights effort, ablaze in the city for six or seven years, was a critical factor. Downey rode its momentum, unencumbered by public association with its more factious elements.

Ironically, by the time Downey took his council seat, the movement's unbridled zeal was abating, or at least changing form.

While the inferno raged in people like the Olivers, Buddy Daye, and Joan and Rocky Jones, and vast amounts of energy would be extended for many years yet, such a frantic struggle could not be sustained. In a public sense it appeared to reach its apex with the Black Panthers' visit in 1968. A direct outcome of that visit, the Black United Front, illustrates this loss of vigour.

By the mid-1970s BUF was not meeting its mandate as an umbrella organization for existing black groups. While it helped carve some economic and political inroads, it struggled to find a clear identity. A rising number of Nova Scotian blacks were coming to regard it as ineffectual.

Yet the period bore significant progress for blacks in the city and across the province. "It raised the political conscientiousness all the way around," says Rocky Jones. "Did we change any fundamental structures? No. I don't think so. But I think we succeeded in changing some of the conditions so that different things could happen to reform the system."

He cites achievements such as the birth of the human rights commission, human rights legislation, more blacks in the police and fire departments and more equitable employment practices.

"I think we succeeded in humanizing the black personality so that people were not able to just disregard the black presence. Prior to this we were almost invisible. We were not part of the political process, we were not part of the economic life except as hewers of wood and drawers of water. We didn't have any influence at all. But because of the kind of confrontations that we had, it forced the power brokers to deal with the moderates because either they had to deal with the moderates, or they had to deal with us. They had to deal with *someone*.

"So they were able to set up these black groups, like the black educators, the black business initiative — all of these groups that bring black people into the system or make the system interact in a more genteel way with the black community. They came about only because we were there. We forced them."

As his brother Graham was riding the crest of a political wave, David Downey's career was in a trough after his loss to Lawrence Hafey. He was faced with a decision — to retire or not to retire.

"A fighter is as reluctant as any other artist to accept the evidence of his own disintegration, even though it's presented to him much more forcibly," American boxing writer A. J. Liebling once observed in his classic *The Sweet Science*. "Between fights he is brisk, active, and lusty, since he is still a young man. He therefore refuses to believe his first couple of bad fights, and blames them on negligence; he has not, he thinks, taken the opposition seriously enough. Then he will lose one or two that he will blame on bad decisions."

Downey felt the loss to Hafey was a bad decision. While family and friends agreed, many suggested it was time for him to retire. Now 34, Downey, always his own man, chose to continue.

His renewed quest for the middleweight championship was aided by an Air Canada employee named Roy Hamilton, who had helped him here and there over the years. According to the *Chronicle-Herald* Hamilton would carry the title of co-manager. He developed a three-bout plan, a renaissance for his fighter to ultimately force a rematch with Hafey.

The first step was a tune-up bout. Selected was Montrealer Gerard *'Le Bull Mean'* Bouchard. In boxing circles many felt Bouchard a "tomato can" — a safe, unskilled opponent who would lose often and frequently take bad beatings in the process. the *Gazette*, more diplomatically, said he was "a boxer without title pretensions." Hamilton and others, however, failed to appreciate that Bouchard had come upon his own renaissance. He was undefeated in his previous nine matches and appeared rejuvenated under his new manager George Drouin, also of Montreal.

The fight took place in August 1976 at the Paul Sauvé Arena in north-end Montreal and ended in the middle rounds with Downey outside the ring, flat on his back, Bouchard on top of him. Bouchard had charged at him football-style, sending first Downey, then himself through the ropes. When Downey tried to rise from the concrete floor, he couldn't move. He was taken to hospital directly from ringside, on a stretcher, his face contorted in agony. The match was eventually declared no contest.

Tests on Downey's back showed no permanent damage. Within a week or so, the only vestige was a slight soreness — and the unresolved issue of retirement. Despite increased pressure to quit, Downey elected to go on. A rematch with *Le Bull Mean* was set for January 1977 at the Halifax Forum, staged by Lawrence Hafey's manager Jerry Fraser and his Red Carpet Promotions.

The career that confounded ended with clarity.

At 2:42 in the eighth round, Downey lay on his back, in the corner of his foe, his eyes open, his legs lifeless, as referee Herb McMullan counted directly above him. Until this point, Downey had commanded the fight. But in the eighth Bouchard caught him with a right. Then a left. Downey collapsed. "I didn't run out of gas," he recollects. "But my elastic broke in my pants, my trunks.

He caught me when my pants fell down. There I'm trying to pull my pants up and he hit me."

Downey said he experienced "a feeling I'd never felt before. It felt like everything from the top of my head just dropped. I asked doctors, 'What does a feeling like that mean?' They couldn't tell me. But it told *me* that it was time for me to get out."

Downey sat on a stool in his corner for a minute, then walked to ring centre where he requested the microphone. "I just want to say that this is the end for me, this is my last fight," he told the departing spectators. "I'd like to thank all the people who supported me through the years and came to my fights. And now I'm going to help my nephew and others with their careers. Thank you very much."

The crowd applauded.

Downey then left the ring, a beaten fighter, an intact man.

Requiem for a champion was part lament, part augury.

"[Often] his bouts were few and far between," Ace Foley wrote. "Well built and with legs meant for speed, Downey had a lot of natural talent. His critics say he didn't use it often enough to gain the heights he felt he would reach before he called it a career. For many years Halifax was regarded as a boxing stronghold, but it was often inactive for long periods during the Downey era."

Hugh Townsend was more approving. "Having to contend with hometown crowds that were sometimes hostile to him, having to stand up for what he believed in regardless of what the public or the media said of him, Dave Downey proved he was an outstanding athlete.

"There was no longer any use, at his advancing age, to attempt a return to the pinnacle. And he was man enough and smart enough to admit it in front of the 2,700 fans who paid their way into the building, many of them hoping to cheer him to another triumph, many others there hoping he would be beaten.

"But it is, in many ways, the end of a boxing era in this province."

David Downey's boxing career was an erratic expedition of fits and starts, at moments farcical, at moments grand, devoid of a clean, progressive arc, haunted with the perception of talent squandered.

So why did such talent not result in greater success? There are several interrelated reasons.

First, it was the wrong era. Undoubtedly there were more rewarding times to be a prizefighter. Starting in the early 1960s and moving into the 1970s, professional boxing was increasingly irrelevant to a public with expanding entertainment options and a pantheon of social concerns in which boxing had no logical place. Hometown sports heroes gradually regressed in the popular consciousness, replaced by distant, temporary celebrities found on the television screen. Only at its highest level — and then largely because of Muhammad Ali — did North Americans notice or care about boxing. The fight game always carried a stench. Now it was suddenly dated and archaic.

Second, Downey's decision to stay in Halifax rather than move on to a larger centre was a poor one. He says his loyalty was strategic — he had a following in Halifax. Many around him felt this was short-sighted. Granted, in Halifax boxing retained at least some status. But even a city with deep-rooted ties to the sport struggled to find reason to pay attention. A paucity of skilled Canadian fighters and a dearth of competent local promoters meant a steady decrease in the number and quality of cards. Those who did come forward to promote tended to be dreamers, not businessmen. Amateurish public relations and slapdash accounting practices prevailed. As a result, no promoter at the time was able to present back-to-back successful cards.

"He could have moved on to be a world's champion," says brother Graham, "but he didn't have the gumption and the guys to get him out of here. You *had* to get out of here. When you are in the game, you have to make the decision. I think he missed the boat by not moving on."

Third, the man he followed as Canadian middleweight champion was Blair Richardson — an unparalleled media darling. Downey never made peace with life in Richardson's shadow. "I think that there was a great resentment — I *sensed* there was — in the way the media responded to Richardson and the way the media probably generally responded to Dave," says Pat Connolly. "I think [he] wrongly interpreted it as a colour thing."

Fourth, there *was* the colour thing. During such a socially tumultuous period in an essentially segregated city, to argue that his race did not impede Downey's career would be beyond belief. He began to box while local publications still described black fighters as "dusky warriors" and "darkies," and reached his peak with Upper Canadian sportswriters referring to him as "the Halifax Negro." Two of his most important fights generated riots with unmistakably racial overtones.

Concedes Harris Sullivan, "I never thought it was that big a deal that Blair always seemed to get more attention than Dave ever did. Part of it was Dave's own fault. Yet at the same time, there *was* the dynamic of racism involved. There was always a built-in sort of bias towards a great white fighter."

Fifth, Downey's relationship with the Halifax media was complicated and prickly. Both factions clung to expectations that the other would never fulfill. Downey sought the respect, deference and acclaim he assumed should be accorded a Canadian middleweight boxing champion. When it did not appear he withdrew, becoming resentful — some of his friends say bitter — as the years passed.

The press expected Downey to fight more frequently. If he could spill some blood doing so, all the better.

Indeed, for a career that spanned 16 years and eight months, there were just 30 recorded matches. In seven and a half years as Canadian champion, he put his title up just five times — successfully defending it three times, losing it the other two. Compared to Kid Howard and Blair Richardson, these numbers are exceedingly low. For this, Downey faced constant, harsh criticism in the media. From time to time writers delicately mused about *why* he was inactive, but never burrowed to really find out. So the Downey enigma endured.

"I think what frustrated a lot of people about Dave was that he had all the essentials, all the basic tools to be a possibly great fighter," says Connolly. "He was a classic boxer who moved very quickly for a middleweight. Good punching power. The guy was capable of taking people out with either hand when he was in the mood to do it. And he was not always in the mood."

Finally, there was Downey's cautious and circumspect personality. Shaped by a childhood typical of the economic underclass in post-war North End Halifax, he had grown to worship the virtues of control. Downey also came to believe — perhaps correctly — that one's own instinct was usually the best. He accepted counsel from few and passed everything through his own dense filters, mirroring the *modus operandi* of his idol Sugar Ray Robinson, who walked alone and who never permitted the world to understand him. Downey's wariness frustrated those who tried to do business with him, be they boxing people, journalists or civil rights activists. It also caused him to move slowly on promising opportunities.

This desire for autonomy determined his inner circle — men over whom he had domain and who would not strongly contest his decisions. Vince Hennebury and Murray Langford were content as a malleable manager-trainer collective that seldom challenged Downey's authority. Control was also a prime reason why he remained in Halifax throughout his career. Although he well understood that Halifax was not the fight city it once was, Downey rationalized at least it was a place where he knew all the players. And those players — rightly or wrongly — believed they needed him. He would not have had such leverage in Montreal, Toronto, Boston or New York.

It is hardly fair, however, to judge Downey's career solely on unfulfilled potential. Granted, he obviously failed if the goal was to be middleweight champion of the world, or even a top contender. But these were designs others assumed for him. He had another blueprint in mind.

While he spoke periodically about rising in the world rankings, this in truth seemed neither his impetus nor his incentive. Downey was palpably fulfilled — and extraordinarily proud — just to be Canadian champion. It was an achievement in which he gloried, even if others did not. It occasionally produced a mention in the national press and certainly afforded him prestige within his community. "Dave was one of our last touchable heroes," says life-long

North End resident Mark Daye, who grew up during Downey's championship years.

To retain this status he had only to retain the title. So, having accurately assessed national regulatory bodies as ineffectual, he fought infrequently and avoided the risk to his title as well as to his health. He also demanded purses dearer than promoters were prepared to pay. If all this made him less popular in Halifax than would have been the case had he engaged in bloody, brain-numbing wars 10 times a year, then so be it.

While this strategy perplexed the media and the boxing community, it also shielded him from the exploitation endured by other fighters of his generation, many who had neither the control nor the courage to defy the system. In the end, unlike Dixon and Langford and Howard and Richardson, all of whom had ring accomplishments he would never equal, David Downey survived a lengthy career as a professional boxer.

Reflects Tom McCluskey, "He more or less watched himself very closely. *'I'm not gonna come out of this game all beat up, I'm not gonna come out of this game stumblin' all over the place.'* Which is very smart. I take my hat off to him, but at the same time I wouldn't take my hat off because he didn't produce the way I liked him to produce, as a trainer. But as a fine family man the guy is sittin' back and I'd say that's the way he *wanted* to live and that's the way he *did* live."

And almost 30 years after his last punch, and more than 10 years since his pensioned retirement from his government job, Dave Downey still smiles brightly, speaks clearly and walks sprightly around his city where friends and strangers continue to come up and shake the hand of a Halifax champion.

EPILOGUE

On the evening of October 28, 1999, the great preoccupation of David Downey's life was soothed when he was formally inducted into the Nova Scotia Sport Hall of Fame. The event occurred in the World Trade and Convention Centre in downtown Halifax before friends, family and media. For the fighter who never felt completely appreciated by the only city he ever called home, it appeared worth the wait.

As time for the formal ceremony neared, the seven 1999 inductees queued outside the door of the Port Royal Room where

David Downey's induction into the Nova Scotia Sport Hall of Fame, 1999.

the festivities would unfold. Third in line was Downey, then 57, resplendent in a black tuxedo, red bow tie and red rose in the lapel.

"He's lookin' sharp," a passing stranger announced to no one in particular, nodding in the fighter's direction. Downey responded with a broad, quick smile.

As minutes passed Downey began displaying the fidgeting mannerisms of a prizefighter about to begin the long walk from the dressing room to the ring. Unconsciously shifting his weight from one foot to the other, taking furtive deep breaths, rubbing his palms together, lightly touching his lips.

The pageant finally began. Applause cascaded from all sides as the inductees marched through the doorway, up the centre aisle into the Port Royal Room, and took their seats. After the crowd settled, youthful CBC sportscaster Bruce Rainnie, the evening's master of ceremonies, offered a 'teaser' about each inductee. Downey's was the most loaded. "He may not have got the recognition we wanted, but we are going to change all that today."

During the formal introductions, Rainnie enthused about Downey, his family, his career and his first professional fight "at 15, in 1957," repeating an inaccuracy that has accompanied the fighter for four decades — Downey was really 18 and the year was 1960. Rainnie followed this with some curious arithmetic, recounting how Downey won the title in 1967, then lost it for the second and final time in 1975. You should be proud, he smiled, "having held the title for *11 years*."

On stage Downey was given a 20-second ovation and presented with a plaque by long-time referee Bobby Beaton, a fellow Hall of Famer. He then strode across the stage to Rainnie for a brief question-and-answer session.

Why did you choose boxing?

"I didn't choose it," Downey smiled. "I guess it chose me."

Laughter. Rainnie beamed and asked a few more genteel questions, all of which Downey handled smoothly. He then looked into Downey's eyes and proclaimed Nova Scotia "a special place."

"Nova Scotia *is* a special place," the fighter agreed. "This is my home. This is where I stayed."

Downey returned to his seat, convoyed by another ovation.

The next night more than 100 friends and family gathered at a local Legion hall to celebrate. Organized by Marlene Bartlett, a warm and intelligent woman with whom Downey had been romantically involved for many years, the evening heard a succession of often-touching testimonials and anecdotes about the boxer and his old neighbourhood. Dressed in the same tux he had worn the night before, but in an ambience more relaxed than that of the Port Royal Room, the honouree grinned the entire four hours.

Such events are high points in a low-key and agreeable retirement made comfortable for Downey by a civil service pension, familiar surroundings and long memories of North Enders.

Through the years Downey has received numerous tributes. In 1974 he sat on the dais at the prestigious Kingsmeadow Sports Dinner, joining celebrities such as Ferguson Jenkins and Gordie Howe. In 1982 his bust was placed in the local Black Cultural Centre. In 1984 he received an amateur boxing award. In 1989 he received a community recognition award. In 1992 he was recognized during a night honouring local black achievement.

And there are other treasured memories. Almost two decades after Downey's 'sparring' match with Muhammad Ali in the lobby of New York's Waldorf Astoria, Ali, long since retired and stricken by Parkinson's disease, travelled to Nova Scotia to help promote a fight involving Halifax heavyweight hopeful Trevor Berbick. He was invited to Province House. As 'The Greatest' sat and signed autographs, Downey, who had come from work, wondered if Ali would remember him.

Soon he stood beside Ali.

"Muhammad, do you know me?" he leaned down and asked. Ali twisted around.

"He got right up and grabbed me and hugged me," smiles Downey. "And everybody asked why did he do that to *that* guy? And he started talkin' to me. To me!"

Incredibly, Ali reached up and touched Downey's slicked-down hair, kidding him that the last time the two met he wore his hair in an Afro.

APPENDIX

David Downey's Professional Fights

Year	Date	Opponent	Place	Result
1960	May 17	Kenny Chinn	Halifax, N.S.	KO 2
1960	Jun 28	Billy McIntyre	New Glasgow, N.S.	KO 2
1960	Sep 27	Peanuts Arsenault	Summerside, P.E.I.	W 6
1961	Mar 6	Claude Labonte	Montreal, Que.	KO by 2
1961	May ?	Peanuts Arsenault	Summerside, P.E.I.	KO 6
1961	Oct 30	Dookie Munroe	Halifax, N.S.	KO 3
1962	May 26	Al McLean	New Glasgow, N.S.	KO 2
1966	Aug 7	Charlie LeGare	Montreal, Que.	KO 3
1966	Aug 26	Peanuts Arsenault	Summerside, P.E.I.	KO 4
1967	Sep 18	Jimmy Meilleur *	Halifax, N.S.	W 12
1967	Oct 24	Manny Burgo	Halifax, N.S.	W 10
1969	Jul 31	Stu Gray **	Halifax, N.S.	KO 8
1969	Aug 27	Don Turner	Halifax, N.S.	D 10
1969	Oct 2	Valley Valasquez	Halifax, N.S.	KO 3
1969	Oct 24	Ray Christianson	Edmonton, Alta.	KO 7
1969	Nov 20	Dave Dittmar	Halifax, N.S.	KO 9
1970	Jul 9	Freddie Williams	Halifax, N.S.	KO 6
1970	Aug 13	Gary Broughton **	Halifax, N.S.	KO by 9
1970	Dec 18	Gary Broughton *	Halifax, N.S.	W 12
1972	Jun 1	Doc Holliday	Halifax, N.S.	KO 10
1972	Jun 22	Joey Durelle **	Halifax, N.S.	W 12
1973	Mar 31	Tony Berrios	Halifax, N.S.	D 10
1973	Jul 5	Roy Dale	Halifax, N.S.	W 10
1973	Sep 4	Tony Gardner	Oklahoma City, OK	KO 2
1973	Sep 27	Gary Broughton	Halifax, N.S.	W 12
1973	Nov 14	Dave Wyatt	Dayton, OH	KO 9
1974	Mar 28	Terry Hayward **	Halifax, N.S.	KO 7
1975	May 29	Lawrence Hafey **	Halifax, N.S.	L 12
1976	Aug 31	Gerard Bouchard	Montreal, Que.	ND
1977	Jan 25	Gerard Bouchard	Halifax, N.S.	KO by 8

Note: Data compiled from *The Ring Record Book and Boxing Encyclopedia* and newspaper accounts. Other fights may have occurred, but these could not be verified.

* denotes title match
** denotes title defence

W = win
KO = knock out (includes technical knockouts)
L = loss
D = draw
ND = no decision

SUGGESTED READING

On Boxing

Brenner, Teddy. *Only the Ring Was Square*. Toronto: Englewood Cliffs, NJ: Prentice-Hall, 1981.

Brunt, Stephen. *Mean Business: The Creation of Shawn O'Sullivan*. Markham, ON: Viking, 1987.

Early, Gerald. *The Culture of Bruising: Essays on Prize-fighting, Literature, & Modern American Culture*. Hopewell, NJ: Ecco Press, 1994.

Fraser, Raymond. *The Fighting Fisherman: The Life of Yvon Durelle*. Halifax: Formac Publishing, 2005.

Greig, Murray. *Goin' The Distance: Canada's Boxing Heritage*. Toronto: Macmillan Canada, 1996.

Hauser, Thomas. *The Black Lights: Inside the World of Professional Boxing*. New York: McGraw-Hill, 1985.

Oates, Joyce Carol. *On Boxing*. New York: Dolphin/Doubleday, 1987.

Oates, Joyce Carol, and Halper, Daniel, ed. *Reading the Fights*. New York: Henry Holt and Company, 1988.

Remnick, David. *King of the World: Muhammad Ali and the Rise of an American Hero*. New York: Random House, 1998.

Saunders, Charles R. *Sweat and Soul*. Hantsport, NS: Lancelot Press and The Black Cultural Centre for Nova Scotia, 1989.

On Halifax

Erickson, Paul. *Historic North End Halifax*, Nimbus Publishing, 2004.

Erickson, Paul A. *Halifax's North End: An Anthropologist Looks at the City*. Hantsport, NS: Lancelot Press, 1985.

Fingard, Judith; Guildford, Janet; and Sutherland, David. *Halifax: The First 250 Years*. Halifax: Formac Publishing, 1999.

MacNeil, Robert. *Wordstruck: A Memoir*. New York: Viking, 1989.

On Race Relations

Churchill, Ward, and Wall, Jim Vander. *Agents of Repression: The FBI's Secret War Against the Black Panther Party and the American Indian Movement*. Cambridge, MA: South End Press, 2002.

Grant, John N. *Black Nova Scotians*. Halifax: Nova Scotia Museum, 1980.

Henry, Frances. *Forgotten Canadians: The Blacks of Nova Scotia*. Don Mills, ON: Longman Canada Limited, 1973.

Marqusee, Mike. *Redemption Song: Muhammad Ali and the Spirit of the Sixties*. New York: Verso, 1999.

Saunders, Charles. R. *Black and Bluenose: The Contemporary History of a Community*. East Lawrencetown: Pottersfield Press, 1999.

INDEX